From Corporate Security to Commercial Force

From Corporate Security to Commercial Force

A Business Leader's Guide to Security Economics

Marko Cabric

Butterworth-Heinemann
An imprint of Elsevier

Butterworth-Heinemann is an imprint of Elsevier
The Boulevard, Langford Lane, Kidlington, Oxford OX5 1GB, United Kingdom
50 Hampshire Street, 5th Floor, Cambridge, MA 02139, United States

Notices
Knowledge and best practice in this field are constantly changing. As new research and experience broaden our
understanding, changes in research methods, professional practices, or medical treatment may become necessary.

Practitioners and researchers must always rely on their own experience and knowledge in evaluating and using any
information, methods, compounds, or experiments described herein. In using such information or methods they
should be mindful of their own safety and the safety of others, including parties for whom they have a professional
responsibility.

To the fullest extent of the law, neither the Publisher nor the authors, contributors, or editors, assume any liability
for any injury and/or damage to persons or property as a matter of products liability, negligence or otherwise, or
from any use or operation of any methods, products, instructions, or ideas contained in the material herein.

British Library Cataloguing-in-Publication Data
A catalogue record for this book is available from the British Library

Library of Congress Cataloging-in-Publication Data
A catalog record for this book is available from the Library of Congress

ISBN: 978-0-12-805149-8

For Information on all Butterworth-Heinemann publications
visit our website at https://www.elsevier.com/books-and-journals

Working together
to grow libraries in
developing countries

www.elsevier.com • www.bookaid.org

Publisher: Candice Janco
Acquisition Editor: Candice Janco
Editorial Project Manager: Hilary Carr
Production Project Manager: Vijayaraj Purushothaman
Cover Designer: Mark Rogers

Typeset by MPS Limited, Chennai, India

Dedication and Appreciation

Dedicated to my daughter Hanna, with love.

I want to thank Mina Bogosavljevic Jovanovic, PhD, for sharing her vast experience and knowledge in strategic marketing by carefully reviewing parts of the book that address marketing and sales and providing invaluable inputs. I also greatly appreciate the involvement of Javier Espinosa García, MBCI, CRISC, CGEIT, in evaluating parts of this book that address Information Security and tangibly contributing to their quality and accuracy by sharing his immense knowledge and experience through comments, ideas, and opinions.

I am especially grateful to Jelena Dinic for her unconditional support and continuous encouragement. None of this would be possible without you.

Contents

Section III   Organize

Section IV Utilize

Section V Embrace

About the Author

Marko Cabric is a globally operating freelance security manager, consultant, lecturer, and author based in Tel Aviv, Israel and Belgrade, Serbia. He has more than 20 years of top-ranking security experience from Europe, the Middle East, and Africa including the Israeli military and homeland security and as a corporate security manager in several industries. Marko manages, teaches, consults, and trains corporate security clients and business teams on various security matters such as corporate security management, physical security, supply chain security, fraud prevention and investigations, crisis management, business continuity, disaster recovery, and information security. He has established corporate security programs for numerous multinational corporations, especially throughout Europe, the Middle East, and Africa.

Introduction

Now that security awareness is part of being literate, businesses need to speak security if they want to communicate with customers.

Although the understanding of the importance of security varies from enterprise to enterprise, it is usually assessed only in terms of the role that it has in protecting processes and assets and its efficiency versus costs. So, even companies with well-positioned security organizations and well-developed security culture rarely take a step forward to understand the real extent of commercial value that they could extract from their security. Unfortunately, in many commercial organizations, Corporate Security is even perceived as being not more than a "nice to have" service and principally, an unnecessary cost whose financial value is measured mostly in terms of its cost saving potential, as additional financial space that could be utilized in case of need.

This book uniquely approaches the financial significance of security for a business. However, instead of just following the usual path of clarifying its basic role in protecting assets, this book takes the road less traveled by shedding the light on the tangible value that security adds to the business and its core processes. It explains why security is absolutely crucial for any business and where and how to position it in the corporate hierarchy in order to tackle performance. But probably the biggest strengths of this book lie in its capability to guide its readers in understanding the role of security as a commercial influencer and how to practically utilize the convenience of having a security setup in the company so that it would realize its true financial potential. Basically, the aim of this book is to fully reveal the often forgotten financial character of corporate security and present it as invaluable commercial force which it is, or at least should be.

Although one might expect it, this is not a typical book on economics with ready-to-use formulas and figures. Instead, this book aims at tackling the understanding of readers about the logic of the quantifiable significance of security for a business. It explains the nature of security as a vital and valuable ingredient of the product, whether that product is a tangible merchandise or a service, and how to utilize that value so that it significantly influences the bottom line.

Being a strong advocate of security evolutionism, as opposed to security creationism, and believing that security is an essential process that continuously changes and develops instead of being a simple product that can be created, bought, used, and replaced, I start this book by explaining the historical transformation of security from instinct and natural process to a professional effort and economic stimulus. We continue by establishing a clear link between security and economics, both on a global scale and translated to corporate setting. Further on, we thoroughly investigate the commercial role of security and how it supports the key processes and the entire enterprise, influences the perception of partners, clients and consumers, and eventually drives productivity and profits. We finalize by guiding the business decision makers in avoiding the common traps associated with cost saving, outsourcing, and the place and role of the security function in an enterprise, and offer concrete advice on how to practically improve the overall business by correctly arranging, positioning, displaying, and managing security.

The concept of the book might raise the dilemma if the content is best suited for security practitioners, business executives, or marketing and sales experts. Actually, the information presented in the book is crucial for all professionals regardless of their role in a commercial mechanism. Moreover, one of the upsides of this book is that it has the ability to interactively adapt to the reader. So, whether it should be regarded as a security book about business, as a business text on security, as a practical guide, or as a theoretical analysis, depends entirely on the individual reader and his/her approach, background, and preferences.

Marko Cabric

Conceptualize

CHAPTER 1

Commercial Security: The Historical Perspective

FROM INSTINCT TO PROFESSION

In a certain form, security existed since the beginning of life and the instinct to protect it. With the creation of community, the instinct slowly faded and was replaced with logical communal concern. Although we can mostly only guess, as we actually do not really know all that much about ancient communities, security was certainly one of the primary concerns of our distant ancestors. Basically, security gradually became a crucial communal process that was motivated by mutual interest and performed using the seven essential pillars of a security process: people, physical elements, technology, procedures, information, coordination, and communication. Although in quite a primitive, but effective form, our ancestors applied all the core elements of security which are until today considered (but not always practically exercised) essential pillars of a security system. While the head of the settlement was in charge of coordinating the protection efforts of the settlement, every member of the community played a part in its security system which was regulated by simple procedures. Certainly, constant routine and emergency communication between community members was of outmost importance as well timely information about the proximate danger. The physical aspect of security mostly relied on the physical terrain and natural barriers that were only slightly adjusted to increase protection while technology was in a form of archaic defense tools. Moreover, as food supply and security were crucial communal concerns, they were also the elements that have shaped politics. Military, and consequently community leadership, would have been chosen mostly based on courage on the battlefield and hunting successes. Basically, the individuals that have demonstrated higher level of performance in processes that were crucial for the existence of the community than its other members were more appreciated and were certainly properly rewarded.

With the invention of money, security started changing from a process performed by all to a profession performed by few. Being an exclusive

From Corporate Security to Commercial Force. DOI: http://dx.doi.org/10.1016/B978-0-12-805149-8.00001-7

profession it also became a product like any other that can be sold and bought. Basically, now days, if you need security, you shop for it.

> Security transformed from a process performed by all to a profession performed by few.

SECURITY AS A PRODUCT

The moment security became a subject of trade, concern as its precondition started weakening and is quickly disappearing. With the loss of mutual concern, people were not anymore fully involved in security processes nor perceived as the essential element of security. Moreover, communication between all those that are concerned with security came down to communication between professionals, while receiving and passing on information in the integral form of human intelligence transformed from a natural process to a professional effort. We basically started believing that we can plainly outsource concern and all the other elements of a security system by simply buying it from a professional. Moreover, with insurance as outsourcing of risk and with legal instruments as outsourcing of responsibility, most of the remaining elements of security got covered by a big pile of paperwork.

> The trend of outsourcing risk and responsibility covered actual security with a big pile of paperwork.

MONEY AS INSTRUMENT VERSUS MONEY AS THE GOAL

Money is not only the instrument but also the goal. As such, money is not only the element that has transformed security into a profession but also the element that is gradually also destroying security as a profession by pushing commercial security professionals more and more away from classic security toward business. Although not at all a bad trend when properly balanced, security professionals are now required not only to care about security but also about its cost and financial benefits and implement financially efficient solutions and continuously come up with cost saving initiatives. Security in profit-oriented enterprises is closely linked to business and its goals. As such, business acumen is certainly one of the key commercial security competences. Unfortunately, in many organizations this trend has crossed the line. The primary concern of many security professionals basically shifted away from security to finances which in many cases transferred the unique security function into just one of the many functions with the primary mission to save and avoid costs. With the loss of uniqueness, employers cannot anymore see the actual value of security which ironically places the security managers on the top of the redundancy priority list.

> The focus on finances transformed the once unique security function into just one of the many cost saving functions.

Money has not only affected the position of security but also its performance, and not only in corporate environments but also on the level of crucial infrastructure enterprises such as airports and railways. As infrastructural services are moving closer to a corporate mindset of measuring performance through profitability, the level of security is also proportionally declining. Basically, national infrastructure enterprises are expected to be optimized and profitable and are adopting the corporate mindset which leads to saving on security, and consequently increased their vulnerability.

FROM SHOOTING TARGETS TO MEETING TARGETS

It is not only the business side that is to blame for this degradation of the security profession. Security is also to blame for the lack of understanding, particularly due to its traditionally introvert nature. Many security professionals fail to understand that commercial security is far more than just a set of security processes that are physically performed in a commercial environment. Most security practitioners originate from military or law enforcement and they switch to private enterprises quite late in their careers. They do not always manage to successfully match security principles and philosophies with the, usually completely opposed, business mindset and entirely different perspective that require new competences and contemporary skills. Basically, security professionals mostly originate from environments where security is the core process and usually have no prior business experience. When transferring to a profit-oriented enterprise they are overwhelmed with seemingly different priorities, "poles apart" philosophies and opposed perceptions. As such they themselves are often not aware of the added value that security brings to core business that goes beyond the obvious. In many cases, security professionals stay isolated from the rest of the company with no applicable knowledge, tools, real influence, and hierarchical opportunities to educate and direct the business. There are only rare cases of security professionals who managed to successfully bland their security expertise with business acumen without sacrificing one competence for the other. Unfortunately, the reality is that in most organizations security stayed isolated from the business or completely transformed into business. In both cases, we have a paradox that business is in charge of making security decisions instead of security being involved in business decisions. Basically, the involvement of professional security in, for example, decisions concerning sales tactics and marketing strategy, in consumer relations management, in financial risk analyses, and during business to business negotiations is in the domain of science fiction.

> The segregation of security from the business or alternatively its transformation into business lead to business functions making security decisions instead of security functions influencing business decisions.

COST SAVING AS SECURITY STRATEGY

The moment business management became in charge of security strategies, cost, as its primary concern became the decision criteria. In the times when businesses outsource all the support functions and security is often entirely outsourced, we have a crucial corporate process that relies entirely on the price.

When shopping for security we basically encounter the same problems that we also stumble upon when buying practically any product. In most cases, the actual "product", its quality, and its ingredients will be quite different from what was advertised. First of all, security can only be effective as an interactive, multidisciplinary process. However, security companies that we are interested in contracting will depend on their primary service focus, try, and often manage to convince us that the particular element of service that they are offering is actually a complete protection system. Usually, security companies prefer to sell technology than manned guarding services. The reason is simple and also directly related to profit. The vast majority of security service providers offer manned guarding services, security technology, or both. Security companies invest in hiring, training, and equipping the security officers and have to pay severance packages to officers that became redundant when the contract with the client ends. At the end, the extremely low cost of manned guarding services leaves them almost no room for profit. The exception is the large manned guarding companies that employ thousands of security officers and as such manage to profit on the quantity. Of course, cheaper workforce, longer working hours, and saving on training and equipment, and basically on the quality, will only help to generate profits. On the other hand, technology has no overhead costs and offers a much higher reward. It also requires servicing, new parts, and system upgrades that will keep the clients hooked and will over time generate additional profit. Still, for companies that buy security services, choosing technology, people, or both is not the only dilemma. With the focus on price, whatever is the decided model, getting the best deal concerning the balance between the quality and the price is one of the primary security objectives while saving costs with each new contract is the security strategy. Still, although price is almost always directly related to the quality of product and service, it is much easier to establish the link between the quality of technology and its price than between the quality of people and the cost of service. Basically, it turns out that the quality of technology is still to some extent a measure. On the other hand, as the quality of people is much less tangible, while the quantity of security workforce is increasing worldwide, both the quality of manned guarding service and its price are constantly decreasing.

> It is easier to understand how the quality of technology relates to its price than establishing the link between the quality of people and the cost of their service.

One of the main reasons why technology is winning the race is also the difference in accounting between people and technology. Security services are a Fixed Manufacturing Cost (FMC/FME) which basically means that the cost of service is included in the cost of the product and shapes its price while, apparently, it does not add commercial value to the product. On the other hand, technology is an investment that, at least accounting wise, adds quantifiable value to the business.

PROFESSION VERSUS OCCUPATION

While seemingly only linguistic, the actual difference between profession and occupation is enormous, especially if we talk about security. Unlike occupation, profession requires specialized knowledge and it is a career category. A person who engages in a certain occupation does not require knowledge and experience and can quickly change occupations. In this era of massive outsourcing, and consequently the mass production of security services, the line between profession and occupation is disappearing. Basically, providers of manned guarding services have over the years managed to gradually convince their clients that they are actually providers of professional security services and not just providers of unskilled occupational labor. One of the trends that assisted them enormously in achieving that is one seemingly insignificant linguistic difference. By changing the name of their workforce from "Security Guards" to "Security Officers" manned guarding companies were now able to convince their clients that they are actually selling professional services for a bargain price. On one hand, security is one of the fastest growing occupations in the world; on the other hand, security as a profession (with the exception of Cyber Security) is not nearly as popular. This indicates that the occupation is gradually taking the place of profession or, more true, that the distinction between the two is fading. Unfortunately, regardless of any fancy name, employment in manned guarding is, for the majority of its workforce, a matter of necessity and lack of choices and not a result of career aspirations. As such, it is unrealistic to expect knowledge, skill, motive, and consequently, performance.

> Occupational employment in manned guarding is often the result of the lack of other choices.

TECHNOLOGICAL ADDICTION

Not only money irreversibly changed the philosophy and performance of security. Another big multidimensional influencer is technology and its speedy development that caught us unprepared. If we look at the life cycle of millions of years that security has existed in a one form or another, the path from stones and bones to sophisticated technology and overwhelming technological addiction happened in a blink of an eye. The development of technology did not only completely change the way that we conduct business but consequently the risks and the way that we protect from them. The technological development of business brought new risks and the use of contemporary means for committing crime. Crime is not only able to closely follow the changing business models but is often even a few steps ahead with the sophistication that reaches the limits of human creativity and uses the newest cutting edge technology. The focus on the technological outsmarting race naturally left everything else behind. Technology started replacing the physical elements of security, shaping the procedures, defining information as purely technological, and making the security professionals heavily reliant on technology or even redundant. Moreover, the term security is being more and more associated with Security of Information and Communication Technologies (ICT Security) and is even becoming its default connotation. The growing importance of ICT which has become a crucial part of the business is certainly the main reasons why ICT Security is winning the right to be the proud bearer of the security title. Another reason is that opinions are shaped and trends are created using the World Wide Web which is logically more the playground of ICT experts than of traditional security professionals.

> Technology is rapidly replacing all the other elements of security and making security professionals heavily reliant on technology or even redundant.

Case Study—The Case of Collin Powell

The case of the former US Army General and Secretary of State, Mr. Collin Powell is a plastic, but not unusual example of how technology killed the logic and established itself as the decision maker. During his speech to the Economic Club of Southwestern Michigan at Lake Michigan College in May 2006, Mr. Powell recalled one of his traveling experiences during which he underwent a thorough airport security body check. As he explained, following a sudden decision to travel, he made three crucial mistakes: He paid for the ticket in cash, he was traveling without a luggage, and was running late. As the airport security software pointed him out as suspicious, he was taken aside and thoroughly physically examined by a security officer. As technology decided, even the fact that the security officers immediately recognized him did not make a difference.

SACRIFICING RESILIENCE FOR PROFIT: MISUNDERSTANDING RISK

The focus of businesses on cost saving such as the reduction of human resources to the operational minimum, the orientation towards technological solutions for processes, the trend of outsourcing all the support functions, and tendency to get the maximum from resources did manage to simplify processes and cut the operational costs. However, adding to that the weakened fundaments of security and its marginalization, the vulnerability of organizations and the impact of incidents increased while logic and common sense weakened. Basically, the ability of companies to prevent and respond to incidents and ensure business continuity and recovery following a disaster drastically dropped. For example, for companies operating according to the "Just in Time" principle, the loss of cargo that is immediately required for production would result in the stoppage of production and endanger the scheduled arrival of products to consumers.

There is a big difference in the way that security and business understand the term "Risk". Basically, they are perceived as two completely different categories that are only namesakes, for security professionals, overall risk is a security category, for business, risk is a solely financial category. This difference in perception is also one of the main causes of conflict between the two. Basically, security professionals were in the past instinctively determined to prevent their companies from taking any risks while the truth is the risk closely related to profit and businesses must take risks to outsmart their competition by accepting a higher level of financial uncertainty such as being the first to conquer emerging markets or offering services that would be more attractive to consumers. Security professionals have only recently realized that they must support their companies in risky business decisions by properly addressing security threats that usually accompany business risks and strengthen the overall security resilience of the company. However, while once it was the security professionals who did not see all the dimensions of risk, it is the businesses today that fail to see the whole picture and are, to profit, taking much bigger risks by also sacrificing security resilience.

Businesses often sacrifice security resilience in order to profit.

THE QUICK-WIN CULTURE

The focus of businesses on cost saving and cost avoidance together with the orientation toward quick profits and short returns of investment also changed the once strategic nature of security by transforming it into a quick-win process. Security organizations in many companies are struggling to be granted the basic resources while almost all the projects are required to result in cost saving or cost avoidance, must have a short return of investment, and should produce almost instant results. Quick-win has become a popular corporate concept for many reasons. For instance, a top manager will most likely hold a current position for a short period, maybe a few years, before moving to another position. As such, strategies that could take a longer time to generate results are unlikely to be approved by top management. One reason is that the vast majority of strategies, even cost-avoidance strategies, require an initial investment. Having a long-term strategy will practically mean that, for instance, funds were invested in a project during the term of one manager who could only report expenditure, whereas his successor claims the results with no spending. The only way for a current manager to present successful strategies and report good results is to have quick-win strategies. Another reason is the appraisal systems that evaluate the performance of employees on a yearly basis, with control assessment often being performed even on a quarterly basis. Security managers who are also being evaluated by their superiors often need to produce solid results based on short-term goals and appraisal periods, which makes it challenging to create long-term strategies.

> The focus of businesses on cost saving and their orientation toward quick profits and short returns of investment changed the once strategic nature of security by transforming it into a quick-win process.

THE NEW REALITY

At a certain point in history, the major security threats and the responsibility for their resolution were indeed more or less reserved for professionals. However, technology also irreversibly changed that comfort. The technological inventions that improved mobility, and made communication and gathering of information much simpler, certainly made the world a smaller place. Unfortunately, crime and particularly terrorism are also enjoying the same opportunities. The shrinking of distances as the product of globalization suddenly brought a variety of security risks right to the living rooms of ordinary people. Crimes and terror can now be committed from a distance using the internet while fear as instrument of terror marketing spreads instantly through new information and communication channels. However, it is not only crime and terror that have flourished in recent years, political violence around the globe, political and military tensions between countries and their potential severity, as well as intolerance between different ethnic and religious groups have probably reached the highest point in history.

Businesses also enjoy more possibilities and are threatened by more risks. They are now able to easily conquer remote emerging markets and effectively and timely manage their operations from a distance. Companies can basically advertise and sell their products by instantly reaching practically any person on the planet who has a TV or internet connection. In past decades, with the need of businesses to seek new markets and lower production costs in remote places, many of them shifted their operations to developing countries where, in many cases, low operational costs are often associated with poverty and as such carry a big variety and intensity of security risks such as crime, terrorism, and political violence. Basically, new business models increased the vulnerability of businesses that operate on distant locations.

> In many cases, low operational costs are often associated with poverty and as such carry a big variety and intensity of security risks such as crime, terrorism and political violence.

International travel, including long-term and short-term assignments, rapidly increased in frequency and distance and especially of their employees and their families who travel and live in foreign countries as part of their work duties. Business travelers and expatriates are certainly vulnerable to numerous risks ranging from pick pocketing, health risks, and accidents to political violence, kidnaping for ransom, and terrorist attacks.

THE VISIBILITY OF SECURITY: THE MARKETING PARADOX

As security threats started affecting all the spheres of life, people again became aware that security and safety are basic human needs and that therefore satisfying security requires both a personal and global approach and joint efforts. Naturally, as such, it cannot be the sole responsibility of security professionals, homeland security services, or security companies. It is therefore odd that companies that are spending billions of dollars just to understand consumers and are doing basically anything possible to anticipate their needs or even engineer their perception of basic needs continuously fail to notice and use the existing ones and, not only start taking their own security more seriously but use the visibility of their security and exploit the actual need for security of their clients and consumers. One of the more popular methods of marketing is certainly Fear Marketing that is mostly used in political campaigns but also to advertise products and services. The key principle of Fear Marketing is to convince potential consumers that not supporting a certain political agenda or not buying a certain product would have overwhelming consequences. For instance, we all know the popular marketing campaigns that tell us that less hair volume and fading colors of our wardrobe will have devastating effects on our social life. However, on a much larger scale when there is actually something tangible to fear, such as when terrorists perform the first part of a Fear Marketing campaign by executing an attack with a disastrous outcome, business often completely fail to use the remedy as a marketing tool and prefer to stay silent. The answer to this mystery could be another marketing principle that prevents us from advertising improvements as the fact that we have improved something probably means that we were actually not doing it that great until then and that we are basically taking the responsibility for previous failures. It could be the widespread belief that even mentioning of security creates discomfort and deters potential customers. Or maybe it is simply that businesses rely on one of the costliest justification sentences in business—"We have always done it this way". A good way to explain this assertion could be on the example of renown international chain of hotels.

> Regardless of the growing importance of security in practically all the spheres of life, business often stay silent instead of using security as a marketing tool.

Case Study—Terrorist Attacks in a Renown International Hotel Chain

Out of 24 major terrorist attacks against hotels that took place between 2002 and 2012, this particular hotel chain suffered three devastating attacks in Asia, in 2003, 2008, and 2009. The death toll as result of these three attacks alone is 490 out of 1799 deaths which is more than 27% of all the 24 major terrorist attacks against hotels during that period. However, while the company most certainly drastically strengthened the security measures in their hotels following the attacks, it is in no way using the higher level of security in its marketing campaigns to attract customers or even simply to reassure the ones that could have logical concerns. Basically, while there are countless search hits that directly associate this hotel chain with bombing attacks, without thorough research, the mentioning of security on their official website that an average potential customer would easily find refers only to "Secure Booking".

SETTING THE STAGE

In many cases, businesses are not even completely aware of the direct benefits of their security, and are often sacrificing resilience for profit. They will often choose to save costs instead of protecting profit and assets. Basically, while the financial benefits of saving on security are felt immediately and are easily quantifiable, in order to experience the downside of the lack of security, we have to wait for an incident to happen, sometimes for a long time. Moreover, we usually cannot predict its consequences. Unfortunately, the high paced business playground and the need to make business decisions based on tangible and easily quantifiable educated guesses point to the direction of accepting the risks and going with the profit. Moreover, we often comfort ourselves with the "it will not happen to me" justification sentence that has, as such, evolved from being a simple excuse to becoming a mainstream security strategy. As such, it is, in case of many businesses, unrealistic to expect that they would allocate time and invest resources to thoroughly analyze the indirect benefits of their security unless these benefits are quantifiable, undoubtedly commercial, and would substantially increase profits. However, it is exactly the economic role of security and its commercial significance for businesses that go beyond the obvious, as well as the discrepancy between the business potential of security and its actual position that are the main focuses of this book.

SELF-ASSESSMENT/DISCUSSION QUESTIONS

1. Do you comprehend security as primary human need or as a "nice to have" service?
2. Do you think that good security makes your organization more valuable?
3. In your opinion, does security influence reliability and client confidence and is it important for customer service?
4. Is the security function in your organization regarded as a partner to the business or as an isolated service?
5. Do you value business acumen more than security skills?
6. Are important strategic security projects with longer return of investment likely to be approved in your organization or is security usually encouraged to focus on quick wins?
7. Are goals given to the security function mostly focused on optimization and cost saving or on producing actual security results?
8. Are you aware of the role that security plays in shaping the image of the company and its products and services?
9. Do you consider the probability of the higher impact of security incidents and business discontinuity when optimizing processes?
10. Do you believe that you will save costs and improve performance by leaning toward purely technological solutions?

CHAPTER 2

Security and Economics: From Global Causes to Local Consequences

GLOBAL INTERCONNECTEDNESS BETWEEN ECONOMY AND SECURITY

The bond between security and economics is rather obvious. Actually, on both global and local levels and in terms of their interconnectedness, economy is an organism with an extremely bad immune system. It can be severely influenced by practically any happening ranging from simple rumors and light rain to armed conflicts and natural disasters. If we were to categorize the economy influencers according to the speed of impact, severity of consequences, and the time required to recover, security issues will be in the top of all three categories. Furthermore, apart from just being influenced by security, economy is also the primary influencer of security which makes it an almost never-ending game. We should also not forget politics which is certainly an instrument of economy (and vice versa) and, among other tools uses military solutions to achieve goals. When I use the term politics, I refer to official government affairs but also to terrorist agendas whose motives and objectives are still unquestionably political regardless of their Modus Operandi.

> Security issues are probably the most powerful influencers of economy in terms of speed of impact, severity of consequences and the time required to recover.

Globalization has made economies more vulnerable to infections as, due to the overwhelming multilayered interconnectedness, the impact of an incident in one location quickly spreads further. On the other hand, globalization also leads to increased competition as it offers alternative markets to companies and substitutes sources to both businesses and consumers. But, while it does provides alternatives to businesses, the global competition is also the assassin of businesses as there are increasingly less obstacles for consumers to abandon one brand and opt for a more convenient one.

From Corporate Security to Commercial Force. DOI: http://dx.doi.org/10.1016/B978-0-12-805149-8.00002-9

THE INFLUENCE OF SECURITY ON ECONOMY

The influence of security instability on economy is especially visible when we look at countries whose economies depend on one industry which is closely related to security. The most obvious example and the first one that comes to mind is the devastating effects that terrorist attacks in Tunisia had on its economy that is based around tourism. Of course, it is not only the countries that are chronically affected by terrorism that suffer consequences. The Basque region in Spain, France, Belgium, India, and Kenya are just some on the constantly expanding list of countries that were, or are, economically affected by terrorism. Moreover, the economic influence of security flaws spreads fast and reaches far. Not only that security incidents in one location have the potential to seriously damage the local economy but they also affect the economy of an entire region and even influence distant, seemingly unrelated events. For instance, in the summer of 2016, security instabilities in North Africa massively directed vacationers to Greece which allowed it to raise lodging prices.

Naturally, security instability is not only a direct threat to businesses but it is actually more the indirect jeopardies that make a market unfavorable for investment. On one hand security and other particulars that define a market are closely related. Chronically insufficient security almost always goes together with poverty, corruption, poor infrastructure, and inefficiency of state services, including administration, but also police and justice. Together with that, security incidents can be for example directed against state's critical infrastructure which could collaterally damage businesses that use it and rely on it. Naturally, while we can to some extent establish the probability if a certain location is more vulnerable to security issues than others, it is almost impossible to accurately determine when and where severe, even long lasting instabilities will occur. We should just remind ourselves of the civil war in Ukraine, terrorist attacks in France and Belgium, and unrests in the United States.

> Chronically poor national security almost always goes together with the inefficiency of state services, including administration, police and justice.

On a more specific level, security is closely related to Foreign Direct Investment (FDI). Companies that are entering a new market want to be confident that the local law enforcement and justice system will be efficient in discouraging, preventing, fighting and sanctioning security incidents, and fraud and corruption that it may be threatened, or affected by. Of course, believing that we can rely completely on our own abilities to combat threats is naïve, to say the least. For instance, due to numerous reasons, in corporate security, we typically do not have the means to efficiently protect our organization during an ongoing attack. Legal boundaries and good reputation prevent us from being equipped, prepared, and able to effectively respond to a surprising, well planned, well-equipped action against us that is performed by motivated perpetrators that are not limited in terms of regulations or reputational hazards.

> Companies that are planning to directly invest in a new market want to be assured that they will be protected by the local law enforcement and justice system.

THE INFLUENCE OF ECONOMY ON SECURITY

While the impact that security has on economy is quite logical, we do not always think about the influence that economy has on security and how to use this interconnectedness to forecast developments. We have already mentioned that security, economy, and politics are tightly bonded. Actually, it is impossible to efficiently manage local security without understanding its global causes. A good threat assessment always starts with global influences and works its way down in order to establish how it influences local circumstances.

> We have to understand global causes if we want to manage our local security efficiently.

When assessing global indicators, we actually look for trends and happenings that have the potential to affect our processes and our security. We are typically interested in gathering information about the wider geographical area (region) in which we are located or has similar markets. We are especially interested in knowing as much as we can about our industry, what affects it worldwide, and whether it has the potential to become a trend. If we talk about politics, companies get their share of threats from political decisions that were made by their founding states. Numerous worldwide cases of vandalism against American fast-food chains have nothing to do with their food or service but are the expression of dissatisfaction with official state affairs. Of course, in every market, we will continuously asses the political, economic, and social climate (including poverty, crime rates, and crime statistics) and its direction. We will further collect and analyze information that could directly affect our company, its processes, and daily routine such as security developments, economic trends, and political decisions and directions.

CORPORATE SECURITY INVESTMENTS AND HOMELAND SECURITY

The biggest success of Islamic State of Iraq and Syria (ISIS) is that it managed to transform itself from an organization to a movement. Basically, as a movement, instead of relying on its official membership and coordinated military strategies, ISIS's tactics rely on its worldwide network of sympathizers who are willing to independently perform attacks on its behalf. Because of its success, it is unlikely that this model of terrorism will be abandoned in the future. As a consequence, instead of focusing on performing major attacks against hard targets, terrorism is increasingly focusing on soft targets as it requires less coordination, logistics, and planning and will end-up being equally rewarding in terms of immediate damages, but also according to their influence on the economy of a state. So, instead of targeting relatively well-protected governmental targets, terrorists increasingly focus on poorly protected business targets. Consequently, we can say that lack of investments in security on a corporate level influences security on a national level. Actually, the race for profitability is severely damaging the resilience of critical national infrastructure as state run services and public utilities gradually adapt the corporate model of profitability and have to show that they are financially viable and self-sustainable in order to survive. As we know well, saving on security is often the first choice of companies when they want to lower operational costs without directly negatively impacting the product or service. This race for profitability has severely impacted the security of public services such as airports, airlines, and railways as they progressively save on security in order to be able to offer lower prices and increase their earnings.

> State run services and public utilities are gradually adapting the corporate model of profitability which severely damages their security and national resilience.

ECONOMIC MINDSET IN MANAGING SECURITY

When I talk about the economics mindset that is required to effectively manage security, I do not mean only business acumen and financial literacy. This actually refers to the methodology of assessing security influences and predicting their impact in the same way that we would assess economic influencers and how they would relate to our organization. Just like in economics, also in security every happening has a cause whether it is direct or indirect. Criminology teaches us that there are three elements that are necessary to commit a crime—motive, opportunity, and means. Actually, these are the three elements that are necessary to perform basically any activity. Consequently, an effective security system invests efforts in understanding motives, limiting the opportunity, and obstructing the means.

> An effective security system invests efforts in understanding motives and causes of crime, limiting the opportunity and obstructing the means that are required for it to happen.

Motive

It would be impossible to list all the possible motives for committing crimes as they could be as puzzling as human imagination. If we are talking about property crimes, usual motives are poverty, greed, envy, desire to cause harm, etc. However, when we assess all the probable motives that could affect our organization, we realize that there could be many motives that do not necessarily have something to do with gain. For instance, the motives for targeting our organization (physically, cyberattack, attack against reputation, etc.) could come from political, economic, queasy-religious, and social agendas that are opposed to our industry or specifically our company, its product, national origin, and programs. Certainly, motive is related to manmade actions. The counterpart of motive when it comes to Force Majeure is cause. As much as we work on understanding the motives of manmade actions, we attempt to understand the causes of natural factors and unavoidable circumstances, establish patterns, and anticipate events. For instance, in Business Continuity Management and Disaster Recovery, we do not regard natural disasters as simply unforecastable and just wait for them to happen. On the contrary, we continuously work on associating the manifestations of nature with regions and seasons. Logically, we can relatively accurately know the period of the year when there is a higher possibility that heavy snow will obstruct our supply chain or the season that carries a higher risk of floods. On top of that, natural factors are also known to influence manmade motives. The "Heat Hypothesis" in psychology states that hot temperatures can increase hostility, aggressive behaviors, and crime rates. Actually, some theories warn that global warming may increase the numbers of violent crimes worldwide. Some institutions, such as prisons and schools, actually use microclimate controls in order to reduce aggression-related problems.

Opportunity

Like motive, opportunity is also a multilayered category. We can explain one dimension of opportunity as ease of access. For instance, not protecting a valuable item gives the opportunity to a criminal to access it. In this case, we could explain opportunity as exploited vulnerability—our vulnerability is their opportunity. When we talk about natural disasters, our failure to protect from them (our vulnerability) would certainly be their opportunity to cause harm. Still, in case of manmade actions, the opportunity to commit a crime does not depend only on physical access. The broader explanation of opportunity would be that it is the ability to commit a crime without being prevented, detected, and/or suffering consequences. In this case, the efficiency of law enforcement and the justice system also have a say in increasing the opportunity to commit a crime. Apart from the threats that arise from the inefficiency of the local justice system, some governments may intentionally violate the rights of foreigners as they would suffer less political consequences than if they were to prosecute their own citizens, lobbyists, and contributors. Consequently, courts may openly or secretly favor their own nationals which would severely endanger the tangible and intangible property of companies, their reputation, and their contracts. Basically, companies that are interested in directly investing in a foreign market thoroughly investigate and analyze the political and economic stability, purchasing power, infrastructure, efficiency of the local administration, effectiveness and objectivity of the justice system, just to mention a few. Apart from the importance of these elements for a business, they are also of interest to security as they influence motives and create opportunity to commit a crime and are a crucial part of security assessments. On the other hand, opportunity can also be a very practical category that does not only depend on our vulnerabilities or global factors. If we take armed robberies as example, statistically less robberies are committed during harsh weather conditions as there could be circumstances that would prevent the criminal from efficiently escaping the scene of the crime. The same goes for regular traffic jams in certain areas and times of the day.

> We can explain opportunity as the ability to commit a crime without being prevented, detected, and/or suffering consequences.

Means

As much as limiting opportunity to commit a crime requires investments, detecting, and obstructing the means that are necessary to perform an action also relies on having the means that will assist us in doing it. Means that are used by a criminal range from information about a target to actual equipment that will be used during a crime. So, preventing a criminal from executing a crime requires both physical security and information security measures that will make it more difficult to collect information, gain access to physical space or systems and networks, and use our infrastructure and equipment as means, or bringing-in his/her own in order to efficiently perform an action. For instance, every employee with access to company's networks has means to inflict damages. On the other hand, many security systems wrongly only concentrate on the means and not on noticing malicious intent. We can often see airport security personnel who act only as logistics support to metal detectors and x-rays without paying any attention to suspicious appearance and behavior.

TRADE AND PEACE

Many years ago I had an interesting informal conversation with a CEO of a US chain of convenient stores who was interested in expanding his operations to the Balkans. He explained that his main criteria for entering a new market is the direct presence of major US companies, especially fast food and retail chains in the market and the fact that they are operating with success. He called his assessment method "the Mc Donald's Assessment" after the popular chain of fast-food restaurants. Basically, the main assurance that he would be fairly treated by official institutions is the amount of trade between his county and his host country. Acceptance of the American fast-food culture also reduces the probability of hate crimes and nationalistic incidents. His strategy is actually based on the hypothesis that says that the more countries trade with each other, the less likely they are to fight with each other. On top of that, instead of investing valuable time and resources in performing a specific and detailed threat assessment, he would rely on threat assessments performed by companies that had previously entered the market and trust their decisions to establish local operations.

However, this strategy does not take into account several very important elements. Firstly, it completely neglects the possibility of suffering the consequences of conflicts even when not being directly involved. The civil war in Ukraine was the result of animosity between Ukraine and Russia but has still impacted all the foreign businesses in the country regardless of their national origins. Secondly, the overwhelming amount of trade between Ukraine and Russia did not prevent the hostilities between two countries but was actually indirectly the cause of the conflict and certainly made the consequences worse. Another threat is protectionism, and not only in terms of official measures but more as a mindset. It could be exactly the amount of trade that could cause the unfair treatment by official institutions, hostilities, boycott, and subsequently losses. Finally, it would be completely wrong to assume that a threat assessment performed by one company would be sufficient for all the companies from the same country that are planning to enter the market. Threats do not only originate from nationality but are actually a fine combination of specific circumstances, such as product and service, agenda, size, visibility and recognizability, affiliation, reputation and precise location, just to mention a few. For instance, during all of the past anti-US protests in Belgrade, Serbia, downtown Mc Donald's restaurants were unavoidably vandalized by protestors. However, protesters never showed any interest in attacking the KFC restaurants that are located just around the corner.

ECONOMICS OF TERRORISM

When we talk about the economics of terrorism, besides the obvious economic consequences that are inflicted by terrorism, we have to also understand what socio-economic factors cause terrorism and how terrorism and economics influence each other. As for the causes, most conclusions rotate around the influence of poverty, inequality, and lack of opportunities on the appearance and growth of terrorism. Consequently, a frequent scholarly approach to reducing terrorism concentrates on improving these conditions. Paradoxically, most imposed measures that are intended to disrupt financing channels of terrorist organizations are based around economic sanctions against states that are believed to support terrorism instead of addressing its root causes. For example, it is believed that the biggest mistake that Israel is making in its attempts to tackle Palestinian terrorism is not its security strategies but the failure to recognize and address poverty as its main motive. On the other hand, it is also very naïve to assume that it would be easy to directly address poverty in hostile countries without taking a serious risk that any economic aid would be misused and eventually backfire.

> Most scholars link poverty, inequality, and lack of opportunities with
> the appearance and growth of terrorism.

Terrorism is not only caused by economic factors but also changes as result of economic influences. For example, the 2007 Global Economy Crisis influenced the transformation of Al-Qaeda in the Islamic Maghreb (AQIM) from just one of the terrorist organizations that are operating in North Africa to one of the wealthiest terrorist organizations in the world. As result of the Global Economy Crisis, states that were pursuing their strategic goals by financing terrorism were forced to tighten their belts. So, instead of relying on subsidy, AQIM transformed from a purely terrorist organization to a synergy of crime and terror that is able to finance itself through drug and people trafficking and ransom kidnapings of foreign nationals who are visiting or working in North Africa.

Terrorism is also far from being only an ideology but is also a very profitable business. It is not a secret that the ISIS bases most of its wealth on exploiting the natural resources in areas that are under their control and undisturbedly selling them outside the territories that they hold. Naturally, the global lack of cash and natural resources forces many businesses and even governments to turn a blind eye to the origin of money and resources that they depend on and recklessly, and often even intentionally, assist terrorist organizations in washing dirty cash and moving it through official channels and toward seemingly legitimate investments.

> Terrorism is not only an ideology but also a very profitable business.

THE ECONOMIC ASPECT OF PROTECTION

Businesses are usually addicted to challenging investments in security only against the direct damages that they might encounter as a result of insufficient security. For example, if we count the direct losses of all the terrorist attacks worldwide during a certain period, we will notice that it is incomparably lower than the direct losses that are the result of traffic accidents during the same period. However, while the cost of a traffic accident pretty much stops at the moment the accident was over, the impact of a terrorist attack continues long after it was finished, while its costs continue to multiply and accumulate. Absurdly, we often base our protection strategies on occurrences that carry a lower risk of damage and consequently invest less in protection in terms of attention, setup, and actual funding. Even when we do invest in protection, we mainly use measure that can stop an incident or prevent its actual realization when the intent to cause harm already exists. Basically, even in security jargon, prevention means stopping an incident at the earliest possible stage, such as during the collection of information about a potential target or during the phase of planning an action. That implies that the intent to commit a crime already exists. We usually do absolutely nothing to address the root cause of potential incidents.

As we have said, everything happens with a reason and both "conventional" crime and terrorism have deeper causes. Naturally, as a corporate entity, as there is not much that we can do to independently successfully address the cause of global terrorism, we should leave it to governments and homeland security organizations while assisting them by cooperating and not turning a blind eye, and especially not facilitating terrorism. Moreover, we should do our best to join the actual protection efforts that are intended to increase the practical security of our organization, community, and region. Still, apart from classic protection strategies, we can improve our security also by addressing the root causes of crime in our community through social development. Crime prevention through social development (CPSD) is actually an economics-like approach to tackling crime that is for businesses unfortunately still a road less traveled.

> We can improve our security by addressing the root causes of crime in our community.

Crime Prevention Through Social Development

As entrepreneurs, we do not only have responsibilities when it comes to the social development of our community but actually need a developed community in order to prosper. A developed community will not only be safer but will also be a better source of skilled labor and financially viable consumers. Many times, companies that do understand the benefits of interacting and participating in the development of the proximate world outside their walls opt for an elitist model of giving back to the community by only hosting cultural events such as concerts and exhibitions and sponsoring sports teams and events. While this model of investing does give results when it comes to visibility, reputation, and good press, it does absolutely nothing for the parts of the community that really need help and where it would produce the best results, both for the community and for the company.

> A developed community is a better source of skilled labour and financially viable consumers.

The direct role of CPSD is to address the local root causes of crime, such as preventing delinquency, by ensuring a better quality of life for the community and specifically addressing the underprivileged part of its population. Typical elements of the CPSD strategy include opening youth centers, offering scholarships, investing in schools and kindergartens, organizing projects with the local community (such as removing graffiti and cleaning the area), and supporting youth in their ideas and initiatives (for instance investing in a skateboard park). It also includes prioritizing the members of the local community when it comes to announcing available vacancies and paid projects and making internal sources, such as company library and gym available to community members.

While many companies require that their security personnel have no connections with the local community in order to minimize the possibility of internal—external frauds and crime, some companies on the contrary exclusively recruit manned guarding staff locally. While there are risks associated with recruiting security personnel locally, there are actually many more benefits, such as ownership, establishing local connections, and developing the community. On top of that local security staff know the routine of the place, have access to information, and have more collaborators, and consequently more eyes in the neighborhood.

Efficient CPSD relies on the ability to understand the needs of the local community and requires frequent contact, not only with the leadership but also with its actual members, especially youth. It also calls for efficient communication with the local police department that can provide a valuable insight of troubles in the area and real needs where information will typically not be shared by the local leadership. Apart from collecting information, an important part of CPSD is transparency, involvement, and openly supplying information to the community about crime prevention efforts through announcements, news, billboards, school visits, and official meetings.

Operating in a socially and economically developed community is certainly rewarding, and not only in terms of security. A favorable social environment, assists the proper functioning of a business on many levels. It also boosts the reputation and social recognition and assists in making the company and its products or services more visible. It will also give a human face to a business.

This sort of networking also does miracles in expanding the network of customers. Finally, practical involvement in the life of the local community will be much appreciated by current and future employees who will appreciate working for a company that makes an effort to assist the neglected and the needy. This will certainly intensify their feeling of pride, belonging, and fulfillment and establish the connection between their efforts and a good cause.

Crime Prevention Through Environmental Design

Crime prevention through environmental design (CPTED) is another interesting approach to crime prevention. Just as CPSD addresses the root causes of crime through social development, CPTED attempts to limit the opportunity for a crime to occur by redesigning the physical environment. Both approaches use development to prevent crime instead of relying only on traditional security strategies to stop it. Instead of using aggressive physical security measures with negative visual impact to deter wrongdoers, CPTED strategies tend to stop offenders from planning criminal acts by changing the physical parameters of the environment. It attempts to limit the practical ability of offenders to execute an action and at the same time address criminal intent by visually improving the physical design and social circumstances. Basically, it uses visually appealing features that discourage crime, while at the same time encourage legitimate use of the space. This does not only make it hard for the criminal to perform an action without being noticed and stopped but also addresses criminal intent. Crime is not only attracted to dark, shady places but run-down areas actually also feed aggressive behavior. Naturally, a pleasing environment is much more calming than an unpleasing one. CPTED is a combination of security, psychology, and architecture and this combination of disciplines is the essence of the concept. For instance, wide, open, and well-lit spaces are uninviting for criminals while they at the same time attract legitimate attendance. CPTED is based on core security principles such as the importance of delaying an action but without using fortress-like obstacles. For example, instead of using concrete barriers to slow down vehicles when approaching the facility, CPTED uses decorative fencing, flower beds, winding roads, and roundabouts.

Although the purpose of this method was originally to address crime on a national, city, or municipality level and not as a security tool that could be used by a physical security system (for instance, a factory) even smaller security systems started applying CPTED as part of the strategies to prevent crime from occurring in or around their facilities. Actually, on a larger scale, CPTED was often labeled as elitist and basically ineffective as it does not stop crime but simply pushes it to poorer areas that do not have the possibility to efficiently address it. On the other hand, it did prove to be very efficient when used as part of a physical security setup of a facility, its immediate surrounding, and neighborhood.

Good security starts with addressing the socio-economic causes of crime, continues by limiting the opportunity for a crime to occur, and continuously works on stopping it through regular security measures. It would be practically impossible to exclusively rely on a single approach to crime prevention in order to produce a winning security strategy as successful security requires understanding numerous influencers and applying a careful combination of many models and techniques.

CHAPTER SUMMARY

Security is closely related to socio-economic factors, both as their influencer and as their consequence and on a large scale as much as on a more local level. Actually, the bond between economics, politics, and security is unbreakable. And still, on the enterprise level where our activities and motives are undoubtedly economical, we usually completely neglect the correlation between economic aspects and security both conceptually and practically. Moreover, in enterprises, we completely unnaturally detach security from business assessments and strategies and remove economics from security strategies and goals. In this chapter, we analyzed how economics and security continuously influence each other but also how sustainable security objectives can be practically achieved through economic activity and not necessarily by only applying traditional security measures. Still, it would be impossible to list and detail all the cases where security and economics meet and to introduce turn-key strategies. Basically, not only that specific circumstances require a tailored approach but methods should actually be regarded only as loose frameworks that provide ideas and knowledge and give legitimacy to common sense, logic, imagination, and innovation.

SELF-ASSESSMENT/DISCUSSION QUESTIONS

1. Does your organization contract external service providers that assess global influencers and forecast how they will influence your security?
2. Do you follow and analyze global security developments that are related to your industry?
3. Is your organization required to follow international security standards and/or local rules and regulations or is it completely free to arrange its security according to its own judgement?

4. As part of your Business Continuity Management and Disaster Recovery, do you invest efforts in forecasting and preparing for specific manifestations of nature, security incidents, and unavailability of workforce that are typical for certain seasons, dates, and events?
5. Do you assess the effectiveness of local law enforcement, administration, and justice system as part of your security risk assessment?
6. Do you have a system in place that is tasked to develop effective relations with the local community and is security part of it?
7. As part of your relations with the local community do you invest efforts in understanding and addressing the local root causes of crime?
8. Do you communicate directly with youth in your local community?
9. Do you use CPTSD techniques to tackle crime?
10. Do you combine CPED techniques with your attempts to visually improve the immediate physical environment of your business?

CHAPTER 3

About Corporate Security: *The Function, Its Philosophies, And Practices*

THE ROLE OF CORPORATE SECURITY

Simply put, Corporate Security is a multidisciplinary and multilayered function whose responsibility is to coordinate the overall security efforts of a commercial organization. In theory, it closely cooperates with the business management and all the functions that are concerned with security, safety, business continuity, and compliance to safeguard business interests, people, profits, and reputation and mitigate risks. It is also responsible for guiding all employees in doing their part in the security system of an organization through their everyday actions and judgments [1].

> Security guides all employees into doing their part in the security system of an organization by exercising secure behavior and judgments when performing regular work duties.

Every Corporate Security Organization is different. It depends on a company's size and complexity, but also on the understanding of the importance of security in a particular enterprise. Security management teams can vary from small teams consisting of a couple of experts to serious security organizations consisting of tens of experts. Functions represented in global security teams consist of managers, each of whom is responsible for a field of expertise: For example, security of facilities (physical and technical security), executive protection, security governance, security trainings, antifraud, business continuity management, and special situations [1]. On top of the regular functions, depending on the industry, risks and scope of the company, there might be other integral industry specific parts of the security organization, such as Retail Loss Prevention. Actually, the role of corporate security completely differs depending on the industry, specifics of the product or service, size and scope of the organization, and distinct risks associated with the location. Naturally, the security organization, including the number of functions, their expertise, experience, expectations, and job descriptions in an oil refinery in Southern Algeria, will be quite different from the team that is responsible for the security of a bank in Geneva.

From Corporate Security to Commercial Force. DOI: http://dx.doi.org/10.1016/B978-0-12-805149-8.00003-0

In addition to their in-house setup, global security teams often contract external consulting services that provide specialized assistance, such as gathering relevant intelligence in potentially risky geographical areas, and managing special situations, such as evacuations from hostile environments and hostage rescue.

Corporate security is in charge of assessing, measuring, and quantifying risks; inventing, planning, implementing, and controlling security measures that are intended to predict and notice trends, prevent and stop incidents, and understand their correlation in diverse parts of the corporation and in different phases of business processes; analyzing the performance and success of security measures and adapting them accordingly while receiving backing from the organization, both in terms of mandate and funding.

Together with knowledge and experience in security, additional key competencies required for a successful corporate security performance are integrity, business acumen, people orientation, management skills, and the ability to effectively communicate and convince the stakeholders to support security strategies and employees to take an active part in them. Apart from dealing with traditional security areas such as physical, technical, and human elements of securing people and property, in some organizations, Security, Information Security, and Business Continuity Management and Disaster Recovery are united under one roof, especially, in the industry of financial services. Still, Business Continuity and Disaster Recovery is usually closely related to Information Security and instead of providing a solution for all the situations that can cause business discontinuity, it usually only addresses risks that are related to the critical Information and Communication Technologies (ICT) infrastructure.

Core security elements of corporate security are:

- Physical and Technical security of people, processes, products, and assets
- Crime Prevention and Detection
- Antifraud
- Information Security
- Security Governance
- Investigations
- Safeguarding the reputation of the company and the brands
- Risk Management
- Business Continuity Management and Disaster Recovery
- Crisis Management
- Duty of Care and Executive Protection

CHIEF SECURITY OFFICER (CSO)

The CSO is a corporate security management position in charge of the overall security of a corporation or one of its affiliates (Group CSO, national CSO, or market CSO). The CSO is responsible for leading the security efforts of an organization through the design, implementation, and management of security strategies and programs based on needs, threats, vulnerabilities, and gaps in order to efficiently protect people, processes, products, and assets. The CSO combines all the security elements (People, Physical Aspects, Technology, Governance, Communication, Information and Control) to develop effective, sustainable, and cost-efficient strategies and lower the exposure of a corporation to financial, physical, and reputational risks. He/She basically controls any risks of happening (Force Majeure), doing (intended actions) or not doing (negligence), for the sake of preventing incidents, managing crisis, and recovering from disasters by reducing their effects on all the elements of a company and ensuring business continuity.

As a senior management role, CSO is, on top of his/her security expertise, required to have business proficiency and to be able to successfully match technical skills with business goals. Adding to the complexity of the role are numerous activities that do not rely solely on security know-how, such as creating and managing budgets, controlling and improving performance (financial, operational, strategical, and human), and interacting vertically and horizontally with all the people that are concerned with security (corporate diplomacy), as well as with contractors, law enforcement agencies, and justice systems. It also often requires managing people and processes who may often be spread over diverse geographical locations and parts of the business. The daily tasks of a CSO consist of both strategic analysis and planning and a reactive (responsive) tactical approach to solving problems. Actually, in reality, the biggest part of CSO's daily tasks consists of responding to issues, even the ones that are not related to their function, rather than engaging in analytics and planning. That is probably one of the main reasons why commercial enterprises do not always manage to keep up with the risks and mostly deal with healing instead of preventing.

> In reality, the biggest part of CSO's daily tasks consist of responding to issues, rather than engaging in strategic planning.

VARIANCES IN SECURITY MODELS IN DIFFERENT INDUSTRIES

As we have mentioned earlier, the models of performing security drastically differ from industry to industry, and even between companies that belong to the same industry but operate under different circumstances. Moreover, even almost identical companies may have completely different security setups as a result of different perceptions of their leadership about the importance of security and the amount of risk that they are willing to accept. When we talk about industries, the three most common types would be enterprises that are based around a product (such as production, the supply chain, wholesale, and retail), the ones that work mostly in the virtual environment and facilitate financial and telecommunication services (such as banks, insurance agencies, various types of ICT providers, etc.) and enterprises that provide lodging and entertainment services (such as hotels and resorts).

> Even very similar companies may have completely different security setups owing to different perceptions of risk and the amount of risk that they are willing to accept.

Risks and Consequences

The industry of financial services functions mostly in the virtual world as the actual physical handling of cash occurs for a limited period of time before it is virtualized. Since the attention and means of criminals changed from robberies and thefts to hacking and fraud, the focus of security on the industry of financial services naturally went to the direction of information and communication technology (ICT) security and fraud prevention instead of traditional security.

One of the main differences between the industry of financial service and Industrial enterprises is the impact and the consequences of service stoppage. Disruptions are typically much graver for a financial institution or for a provider of telecommunication services than for an industrial enterprise. Actually, in the production industry, it is mostly the company that suffers the consequences, and not the consumer. On the other hand, business discontinuity in the industry of financial services can have catastrophic consequences for both the company and the client. For instance, a customer who was in the middle of a bank transaction at the moment the service became unavailable cannot suddenly turn to another provider. Naturally, it would have an immediate impact on the reputation, the confidence of client, and consequently on profit. As for product focused industries, in most cases, the anti-monopoly system grants consumers the ability to acquire the product from alternative manufacturers. So, while the company would certainly lose money due to service stoppage, it would not necessarily have an impact on the client. Logically, the role of Business Continuity Management and Disaster Recovery is much more valued in the industry of financial services than in other industries. In the hospitality industry, apart from the need to protect the assets of the hotel, the main focus of security is on the safety of the guests. While security is one of the most neglected parts of the hospitality industry, in hotels, incidents, such as terrorist attacks, can have immediate and devastating effects, and not only temporarily and solely on the particular hotel but on the entire market and they can be felt for a very long time.

> As antimonopoly systems usually grants consumers the ability to acquire products from other sources, according to the impact on customers, business discontinuity issues are typically much graver for financial institutions than for product oriented enterprise.

Internal Risks

On top of external risks, all three types of industries also face internal risks. Still, the Modus Operandi of internally committed crimes also differs from industry to industry and consequently, so do the security measures that are intended to prevent them, detect them, and stop them. For example, in the production industry, the focus in preventing employee-related crime is on the product. To prevent a product from being smuggled out of the production facility, we concentrate on the physical exit points in the facility. On the other hand, because of its virtual nature, it is possible to remove the product from a financial institution during almost every phase of core processes that involve numerous departments in the front office and back office and many employees, in which each link in that chain could be the exit point. This specific risk in the industry of financial services has led to the development of much stronger internal control functions, such as internal audits, compliance, and operational risk, and the development of more levels of control for employees and processes [1]. In the hospitality industry, the most common internal crimes are employee theft and embezzlement. The consequences of internally committed crimes are minimal when it comes to the assets and property of the actual hotel. However, in cases when the victims of theft and embezzlement are the gusts, the consequences are naturally much more severe.

The Position of Security in Different Industries

One of the obstacles for security in the product-based enterprises is its position. Security is placed where the focus is on the company, usually linked to production and naturally pays more attention to processes in his/her sector than to other parts of the company, even when other processes actually deserve more attention. Even in cases when the company operates with separate legal entities, such as Production Company and Sales Company, it is rare that security be placed under the chief executive officer who is managing for both companies. On the other hand, the security organization in financial institutions is usually in a better position to supervise entire processes.

Moreover, in order to avoid any conflicts of interest, in some financial institutions security reports directly to the group security unit instead of reporting to the local management. Due to the nature of risks, in financial institutions, security cooperates closely with ICT while Information security is usually part of the security department and not of ICT and actually functions as the second level control of the ICT department. On the contrary, in the production industry, information security is usually not united with security. Actually, the two sides of security even hardly ever communicate, let alone cooperate. In such companies, security is usually affiliated with Environment, Health, and Safety (EHS) and sometimes even united with it in the same department. In the Hospitality Industry, security is often part of General Services or Facility Management and in most cases plays the second fiddle. While facility management adds to the experience of gusts, it is often believed that security takes away from that experience. In hotels, security is usually hidden, marginalized, and often does not have a say in core business processes. Naturally, the actual abilities of security closely follow the treatment that it receives.

MISCONCEPTIONS ABOUT CORPORATE SECURITY

While in theory, the role of security in commercial organizations should be quite clear, in practice Corporate Security is probably still one of the biggest mysteries of the corporate world. The role of Corporate Security is often misunderstood by businesses, filled with controversy and overshadowed by internal conflicts [1]. We could even say that the treatment that a security function repeatedly receives is quite similar to that of a soccer coach or politician—everyone that does not do it thinks that they could do it better.

Actually, many managers instinctively value two types of subordinates: those that are their clones in terms of expertise and that could be easily assessed and measured, and those that are their complete opposites and engage in specialist professions that their managers need but are completely unfamiliar with. Unfortunately, security does not fit in either of the two categories. Absurdly, security is an expert function that requires specific and extensive knowledge, skills, experience, and abilities, but the one that everyone has an opinion about and thinks that they know exactly what it should do. Consequently, in many organizations, the security concept is managed and designed by the business function and only executed by the security function. For instance, during performance appraisals a security manager is required to present his/her past achievements and future objectives in a way that the superior understands it without investing too much time and energy in analyzing it. Basically, the goals are actually often even determined by the superior in a way that they match his/her idea about the role of security which rarely corresponds with what security should actually do. Naturally, it is exactly those objectives that shape the protection strategy of an organization. Security is actually often treated like a general support utility instead like a specialist function.

> In reality, security is in many commercial enterprises managed and designed by the business function and only followed by the security function.

Security managers are even frequently assigned tasks and projects that have absolutely nothing in common with their expertise, simply because the project does not directly relate to other functions that are seemingly easier to comprehend or to those that seem more important and are more difficult to understand. Basically, the opinion about security as unnecessary cost leads to security being given various unrelated tasks in order for it to actually become worth the expense. A security guard in a bank branch will spend most of his/her time photocopying contracts, searching the archives, and assisting the tellers and the clients with whatever they might need, instead of performing authentic security tasks. I have also witnessed many situations, even in large enterprises, when senior security managers are being assigned projects such as refurbishment of premises, supervising the gardening in the compound, and managing production waste, even while their companies are experiencing severe security risks and the vulnerabilities are not properly addressed. As I have already mentioned, in many cases, Security Organizations are part of other functions such as General Services, Facility Management, EHS, Engineering, or Human Resources. Naturally, the tasks and the projects that Security is tasked with correspond to the function that it reports to.

> Security managers are frequently assigned projects that don't relate to their expertise, usually when particular projects don't directly relate to other functions that are easier to understand.

Business Acumen

Business Acumen is undoubtedly one of the most important competences of a Corporate Security Professional. Security does not exist to serve itself but its purpose is to be part of the wider context in which business naturally plays the leading role. Business acumen basically comes down to understanding business, its principles and language, understanding the company's specifics and its core processes, being financially literate and being able to align supporting strategies with business goals. As such, Business Acumen appears to be more of a concept than a simple competence as it requires using specific technical knowledge to perform actions while exercising a business judgement. Of course, every concept has to be correctly proportioned in other to be effective. Still, in many cases, superiors instinctively favor business competences as something that they are familiar with over security proficiency that is not their field of expertise. Unfortunately, it proves to be quite difficult for security professional to materialize their purpose and successfully focus on performing actual security tasks while at the same time being positively assessed by the function that they report to and reaching imposed goals. Actually, commercial organizations where security professionals manage to exercise Business Acumen and retain their security expertise are quite rare. The reality is that in most cases, the security function keeps itself, or is being kept, away and secluded from the business, or is alternatively completely transformed into business by discarding anything that made it unique and practically becoming just one of many cost saving functions. With the security function being completely isolated from the business or actual security being completely removed from the focus of the function, it is either way the business that becomes entirely in charge of making security decisions instead of security being involved in business decisions.

> Business Acumen is a concept rather than only a competence as it requires possessing both specific technical knowledge and a business mindset and having the practical ability to successfully combine them.

Changing the Perception

The increase in the frequency and diversity of security risks and their impact on companies is actually forcing companies to reevaluate the traditional opinion that security is not more than a "nice to have" service and an unnecessary cost for the business that should be either used to perform unassigned tasks or made redundant. Commercial enterprises are only now starting to realize that security actually does protect assets and even that it does add value to key business processes and the company as a whole. However, the perception is changing slowly, while the actual practical changes are naturally following even slower. On one hand, the trust and understanding are still missing in many organizations; on the other hand, companies are usually reluctant and heavy-legged when it comes to getting rid of traditions, even when they know that these traditions block the way to improvement.

> Companies often refuse to abandon traditions, even when they block their way to improvement.

Security Convergence

Due to the growing importance of security, some businesses started to realize that Security should not be a part of General Services or placed under EHS but that it is actually a crucial concept that is vital for the entire organization and as such deserves to be a distinguished function. Security Convergence is quite a contemporary trend that attempts to improve the position of security, its influence, and performance by uniting two traditionally separate security functions—Physical Security and Information Security under one umbrella. However, while the principle and its benefits definitely hold water, Security Convergence is unfortunately an example of good intentions gone bad. Instead of simply organizationally uniting two departments into one so that Physical Security and Information Security experts can coordinate their operations and jointly control and manage the overall security risks of an organization, companies are often deciding to choose between one of the two functions, usually Information Security, and additionally assign it Physical Security tasks. Still, while both Physical Security and Information Security have the goal to insure the safety of their organization, they focus on different concepts, use different means, and require quite different competences. For example, one of the common weaknesses associated with ICT security professionals who deal with other security aspects is the tendency to address security by over-relying on technological solutions. Actually, even the principles and strategies of Physical Security and Information Security sometimes tend to contradict each other. For instance, while breaking the routine is one of the most important tools of physical security, for information security not having a clear routine can be more of a disadvantage than a benefit. Also, target hardening which is a very important part of physical security does not at all exist as a concept in Information Security. Basically, choosing one expert and expecting him/her to successfully manage the processes of the other one will result in the big portion of risks remaining pretty much unaddressed or managed incorrectly.

> Security Convergence is an example of good theory turning into bad practice.

Lateral Move

Lots of companies actually decide to take a quite different approach to resolving the traditional misunderstanding between security and business, by moving employees that do not have the appropriate knowledge and experience and have performed unrelated duties to security management positions.

First, by bringing someone from the company that possesses evident knowledge of the business to a position where it is one of the key requirements seems perfectly logical. Second, it can solve the problem of not being able to promote an employee that deserves it (talent pool) and risking to lose him/her due to the lack of suitable advancement opportunities. Finally, a company can save some money by not hiring a specialist. Although to business leaders, this model does tick all the right boxes, it often proves to be a complete failure as the actual performance usually does not contain the security element which is after all the purpose of the function.

CORPORATE SECURITY OBSTACLES AND CHALLENGES

It would be unfair to only blame the business for the flaws in this "arranged marriage" type of relationship that exists between security and business. While there are since not long ago paths to a corporate security career that do not necessarily require army or police backgrounds, many corporate security professionals still originate from military, law enforcement, or national security agencies. These security professionals come from organizations where security is core business to commercial environments with their role being a support function. During the transition from "shooting targets to meeting targets" they are naturally overwhelmed with completely different priorities, philosophies, and incomparably lower budgets. As such it would be unfair to expect that they easily adapt to new conditions. Moreover, unlike in core security organizations where security is instinctively understood and followed without being additionally tested and questioned, they are now required to adjust their traditionally introvert occupation to corporate circumstances and be able to effectively communicate in order to gain any support and achieve performance. Actually, even the business terminology poses challenges. Apart from stumbling upon completely new terms, security professionals find it especially challenging to change their understanding of terms and concepts that get an entirely new meaning when applied to a commercial setting. For instance, one such word, or should we say concept, is "efficiency." For security professionals, efficiency is the speed and success of solving a problem regardless of the cost. However, for a business, for something to be efficient, it must be cost-effective as well. Actually, it is exactly the differences in understanding efficiency that can explain the quite different philosophies and goals of businesses and security and their often troublesome relationship.

> During the transition from 'shooting targets to meeting targets' security professionals often fail to accept different priorities, understand new philosophies and produce expected results with incomparably lower budgets.

CHAPTER SUMMARY

In this chapter I attempted to explain the role of security in a commercial setting. However, the difference between practice and theory is usually bigger in practice than in theory. Basically, when looking at the role of corporate security today, we cannot ignore the obvious discrepancy between theory and practice. If we analyze job announcements for corporate security managers, we might get the idea that companies indeed take their security seriously. Interestingly, criteria of most commercial organizations for the employment of security professionals on leading security positions tend to be very high. Moreover, it is also a very competitive market that consists of a countless number of security professionals with all sorts of backgrounds and skills that all have the career goal to enter the world of corporate security and are competing for a limited number of available positions. This struggle includes racing to obtain all possible related and unrelated certificates and diplomas, keeping up-to-date with risks and strategies and constantly acquiring new knowledge and skills. Unfortunately, in most commercial enterprises, the Security Management function is far from being utilized. Sadly, Corporate Security is often a depressing story about resources, knowledge, expertise, and abilities being completely wasted while many companies ignore limitless potential opportunities that they would achieve by granting security the credit that it deserves. Actually, instead of continuously trying to change security so that it would match their understanding of it, businesses would be much better off by giving security the backing to do what it does best and enjoy the benefits.

SELF-ASSESSMENT/DISCUSSION QUESTIONS

1. Is the CSO in your organization given the motivation, time, and resources to analyze and plan security or is he/she expected to mostly respond to issues?
2. Is the security function in your company positioned according to business focus, actual risks or simply based on organizational convenience?
3. Do you believe that the security function in your organization has the opportunity to monitor and supervise all the key processes?
4. Is the security function in your organization frequently assigned unrelated projects?
5. Are security professionals in your company encouraged to suggest goals that relate to their expertise?
6. In your company, are Physical Security and Information Security related organizationally?
7. Does your company have two specialized functions that manage Information Security and Physical Security or one of the two functions manages both concepts?

Reference

[1] M. Cabric, Corporate Security Management. Challenges, Risks, and Strategies, Butterworth-Heinemann, Newton, MA, USA, 2015, pp. 35–52.

Reevaluate

CHAPTER 4

Risk: *Stuck Between Security and Economics*

THE CONCEPT OF RISK

The wellbeing of any company and its prosperity depend on how successful it is in assessing risk and finding the right balance between risk and reward so that its risk appetites become an advantage instead of being a threat. Still, business decision makers are often one-dimensional when it comes to risk. They usually believe that financial risk and security risk are two completely different concepts that accidentally have the same name. Abraham Maslow has said that "If the only tool that we have is a hammer, we see every problem as a nail." It demonstrates the negative aspects of the tendency to over-rely on the familiar ones and completely disregard the unfamiliar ones. We basically tend to see only one side of a problem and only one way of solving it. When related to our job, we see the problem and the solution solely through the prism of our business function. Although we are mostly aware that we will achieve better results by embracing diversity, we usually manage diversity in a completely wrong way. So, instead of managing Risk by approaching it from different sides, we split it into parts and approach each part separately with a single point of view. We use the term Risk daily. We can think of numerous definitions that describe it and, moreover, base our business decisions upon it. Risk is a term that is actually quite loose as the way that we approach it often depends on our subjective (or departmental) understanding. Basically, risk is both a process and a situation; it is a financial category, as much as it is a security category; it can be both internal and external; it is a driver of business prosperity as much as it is its threat. However, while in order to manage risk, we need to approach it as a complex phenomenon. we tend to split it into pieces, apply the "assembly line" principle and micromanage its parts separately. Certainly, the first mistake that we make is to divide risk into financial and nonfinancial risks. Regardless of the label, all the risks end up being very financial. Basically, we abridge when it comes to labeling models just so that we would be able to manage them

From Corporate Security to Commercial Force. DOI: http://dx.doi.org/10.1016/B978-0-12-805149-8.00004-2

more effectively. Unfortunately, we start believing in the short, general version of the concept and recklessly base our strategies upon it.

> Instead of managing Risk by approaching it from different sides, we split it into parts and approach each part separately with a single point of view.

Financial and Nonfinancial Risks

Actually, businesses are usually only interested in learning about Risks that can have direct financial consequences. Some terms became so strongly associated with financial language that they are by default understood financially. Risk is used in corporate language to explain financial and investment risks. Moreover, the term "risk" became so strongly associated with financial risks that it became its default connotation. Basically, to describe risks in their traditional (security) sense, we wrongly use the term "nonfinancial risk." Of course, "nonfinancial risks" would be something that we will naturally pay less attention to. However, all risks eventually turn out to be financial. As for security risks, we could even go an extra mile and categorize them as risks that are not only limited to financial consequences but that can, on top of its financial significance, cause physical damages, serious disruptions, and even loss of life.

> Security risks are not limited to only financial consequences but can also cause physical damages, serious disruptions, and even loss of life.

Risk Versus Bad Investment

The term risk is typically defined and understood by businesses as uncertainty of a return of investment and the potential for financial loss, which comes down to risk being just another term for bad investment. Actually, probably the biggest mistake that we make is that we see loss as proportional to investment—the more we invest, the more we can lose. Furthermore, we will only pay attention to larger investments. We can take employment as an example. Hiring a senior manager is an investment, but would certainly not be considered large investment. On the other hand, having a bad hire on a senior management position is a serious risk that could cause enormous losses, both directly and indirectly. Basically, a bad hire could, depending on the position, cause direct losses as a result of employee dishonesty, loss of productivity due to the lack of skill or negligence, and impact other risks such as credit risk as outcome of foul play or bad business decisions. Needless to say that such losses would not be proportional to the investment but could significantly exceed it. Actually, as we do not include employment risks in our risk matrix, we often do not approach employment as a process that should reduce risks. To be more specific, we only look at hiring as potential benefit for the company and not as potential risk. Consequently, we mostly focus on expertise of candidates and not on personality factors. It is however exactly the personality factors that will make a difference between a good hire and a bad one. Good background screening practices are actually surprisingly quite uncommon in most commercial organizations. Subsequently, the routine involvement of security in background screening and systematic use of its skills in protecting a company from employment related risks is extremely rare, whether we are talking about junior, mid, or senior level positions and regardless of their sensitivity and influence on the business.

> We often wrongly regard loss as proportional to investment

Actually, an all-inclusive concept such as risk should not be limited by narrow definitions. By simply defining a concept we create boundaries that prevent us from exercising flexibility, logic, and common sense when addressing it. If we would remove the words "financial" or "investment" from our definition of risk, we would come closer to understanding it as a complex phenomenon and approaching it with more depth. We could, for instance, simply say that Risk is the level of probability of harmful events.

> We should refrain from using narrow definitions to explain risk.

RISK MANAGEMENT FUNCTIONS

Of course, no one doubts that it is absolutely crucial for a business to have functions that are directly focused on understanding, identifying, and mitigating risks in their respective field of expertise. The more complex an organization is, the more Risk Management functions it requires in order to address various types of risk.

Security

Security is clearly a core risk management function. Corporate security is a multilayered, interdisciplinary function that requires numerous competences, skills, and knowledge and consequently has enormous potential. However, the truth is that its abilities are rarely completely utilized in the overall risk management efforts of companies. Actually, despite all the changes that the concepts of business and trade have experienced over the past centuries, and especially in the past few decades, the scope of security mostly remained unchanged, mostly owing to the ignorance of the functions that security reports to, and their failure to understand corporate security, its true potential, and its actual abilities. Basically, instead of being valuable business partners, in many companies, security managers are not more than guard commanders. As such, security is often limited to dealing only with traditional security risks which leaves many security, and security related risks unaddressed. Moreover, the only thing that has actually changed in the risk management efforts of security is the tools that it uses, which are becoming more and more technological. However, its influence has pretty much remained the same.

> Despite all the recent changes in the concepts of business and trade, the scope of security mostly remained unchanged.

Security of Information and Communication Technologies

Information and Communication Technologies (ICT) have become a key corporate function, together with Operations, Sales, Finance, and Human Resources (HR) that are the traditional four wheels of business. Its role is undoubtedly crucial in facilitating business processes as businesses completely rely on their ICT systems and networks to perform basically any activities. As a result, risks that are associated with ICT have the potential to have disastrous effects on the company. So, whatever type of risk we are talking about, risks that are associated with the ICT infrastructure are certainly their integral part. Consequently, ICT risk management is an important ingredient of all the other Risk Management efforts.

Operational Risk

The role of operational risk is to focus on risks arising from assets (people, systems, etc.) with which the company operates and to quantify those risks. Basically, operational risk manages the risk tolerance of an organization and the loss it is prepared to accept owing to the imperfection of its assets. It balances between the cost of errors, the cost of correcting the errors, and the financial benefit of the improvements. Operational risk includes, for example, reputational risk (damage to an organization through loss of its reputation or standing) or impact of operational failures, as well as from other events including fraud, employment practices, and work safety, damage to physical assets, business disruption and systems failure, and so forth. Obviously, risks that are the focus of Operational Risk overlap with other risk management functions. However, the actual practical cooperation between Operational Risk and other functions that are tasked to manage risks is often very shallow.

> The coordination of activities between Operational Risk and other risk management functions is often very shallow.

Credit Risk

A credit risk is the risk of default as a result of the failure of the debtor to make required payments. Basically, the main goal of Credit Risk is to ensure the profitability of lends. In financial institutions, security cooperates (or should cooperate) closely with credit risk, especially by performing investigations concerning fraudulent credit applications (external fraud) and approved bad credits that have the elements of internal or internal–external (external–internal) fraud.

Market Risk

Market risk ensures the profitability of an investment in a certain market, such as preventing poor strategic business decisions. Security should provide assistance to market risk by assessing the security and political violence risks associated with the potential investment. It is however exactly the security factors that could turn a good business idea into a bad investment.

Compliance

The compliance unit ensures that a company complies with laws, regulations, and rules. It has a crucial role in preserving the integrity and reputation of the company, especially in the industry of financial services or in industries whose products have questionable ethics. The goal of the unit is to make sure that the company complies with rules set by legislators, regulators, and its board of directors. In financial institutions, antimony laundering, which combats the transformation of crime money into legitimate money and/or assets through regulations and controls, is usually part of the compliance unit. Anti-money laundering also complies with international and national regulations aimed at detecting and disabling the financing of terrorism. Security functions as a field force of compliance that should physically ensure that everyone in the organizations complies with internal and external rules and regulations.

Internal Audit

The role of internal audit in an organization is to ensure a systematic and disciplined approach to processes with a commitment to integrity and accountability. The scope of internal audit activities is wide and often includes compliance with internal and external rules and procedures (governance), effectiveness of operations, and reliability of financial and management reporting. After an audit, internal audit will issue a report consisting of findings and obligatory measures aimed at improving the audited processes and lowering risks. Internal audit also conducts anti-fraud audits to identify potential frauds. It participates in fraud investigations, together with professional investigators, and conducts post-investigation audits to identify control breakdowns, establish financial loss, and impose measures aimed at closing gaps. Although internal auditors are employed by the company, independence and objectivity are the basis of internal audit. This requires organizational independence from the management of the company, which enables unrestricted control of management activities. In most cases, chief internal audit executives report to the audit committee, which is a subcommittee of the board of directors.

FUNCTIONS WITH RISK MANAGEMENT RESPONSIBILITIES

Apart from functions that are specifically tasked to mitigate risks, every corporate function performs risky activities and has risk management responsibilities. For instance, although HR, Legal Department, Environment, Health, and Safety (EHS), Engineering, and Procurement are not namely considered Risk Management functions, they all perform risk management activities and have an important role in preventing and addressing risks that a company might face.

> Every corporate function, whether namely a risk management function or not, performs risky activities and has risk management responsibilities.

Human Resources (HR)

HR has an important role in preventing and addressing risks and often overlaps and cooperates with security in its risk management activities. It is responsible for creating and managing user profiles (availability of tools, benefits, access rights, and right to know and see, based on an employee's function), managing employment processes, including background screening and executing job terminations (creating strategies and assessing risks of job termination, including strategies for massive redundancies), and imposing disciplinary measures and sanctions. HR is also a partner of security when it comes to designing and delivering trainings for employees and fitting the security training into the overall training matrix of the organization. HR and security also work together in designing strategies for travel security and protecting top executives. It also deals with the employee relations aspect of business continuity management and basically designs a strategy to ensure sufficient workforce during a holiday season. HR is also responsible for negotiations with trade unions to ensure common goals and strategies and during crisis situations such as strikes and demonstrations in order to make sure that they have a minimal effect on the business.

Legal Department

The legal department naturally addresses the legal risks that a company might face, including assessing the legality of actions, determining legal responsibilities, preventing a company from taking unlawful actions, and legally protecting it from flaws. It also creates contracts that determine accountability and legally protect a company from external and internal risks. The Legal Department, HR, and security together assess potential legal risks associated with employment and with sanctions against employees. Security assists the Legal Department by creating the default security clause that is inserted into all legal contracts between the company and its contractors. They also together create the nondisclosure agreement as one of the crucial agreements between the company and its internal and external employees and contracted companies which is intended to prevent risks that could arise from data leakage.

Environment, Health, and Safety (EHS)

EHS manages the risks of safety incidents and health issues on people and processes, the risks that company's processes can have on the environment, and the risks of legal implications of the failure to comply with rules and standards. In industrial systems, security is often united with EHS. Even if it is not officially organizationally integrated, security is the field force that monitors the actual practical compliance with safety regulations. In any case, security and EHS together share certain responsibilities, the most important of which is fire safety, in which security, EHS, and the engineering department have a shared responsibility. EHS is also responsible for the health aspect of business continuity management, and together with security, it provides a solution for health threats to employees and their impact on the business.

Engineering

The engineering department (facility management) is responsible for the physical and technical (non-ICT) aspects of the business and for risks and business continuity management associated with critical infrastructure (electricity, water, etc.). Engineering is also the main partner of security in the domain of physical and technical security. In many companies, security is logically and operationally responsible for security equipment whereas engineering is responsible for budgeting, purchasing, installing, and maintaining the equipment.

Procurement

The procurement department organizes and conducts bidding for the purchase of equipment and external services and negotiates the prices. It is an important part of the overall risk management efforts of the company, by both insuring the quality of purchased assets and services and making sure that they do not pose a risk to its operations, and controlling spending. Security for instance assists procurement with the protection of information during bidding processes, ensures that there are no internal conflicts of interest, and, upon request, performs investigations to evaluate participating companies and bidding documentation to prevent fraud.

SECURITY AND RISK

Security was traditionally not included as factor in risk management processes due to its inflexible understanding of risk. Security professionals were logically focused on preventing their companies from taking any risks, without understanding that risk, uncertainty, and profit come as package and that companies have to take risks in order to outrace their competition and prosper. However, over time, security professionals have learned that they should not stop their companies from taking risks, but that they should actually provide support to their organizations by addressing the security dimension of risk that almost always accompanies business uncertainties.

> Security is often not included in non-security risk management processes due to its traditionally inflexible understanding of risk.

Risk Tolerance and Resilience

While it was once security professional that misunderstood the concept of risk and its importance for business prosperity, it is now business that often excludes security risks from its risk estimations and recklessly sacrifice overall security and resilience, and even the very existence of the organization for a bit of quick profit.

Security as Ingredient of all Risks

It is actually security risks that accompany all core business processes and are the elements of all other risks. As such, security should have a say in all the risk management processes of a company. Still, while in theory it does, in practice security rarely cooperates with other sectors of a company in its efforts to identify risks, determine their acceptable level, and minimize their effects on the business. However, security should naturally be a connecting substance of all the separate risks management functions, whether these functions are involved in mitigating risks directly or indirectly, and be a crucial part in the overall risk management strategy and practice of a company. It could exactly be the overlooked security issues that could be the reason for investment failures.

> Security risks usually accompany all core business processes and are contained in all other risks.

Case Study: Retail Pharmacy Chain

A very good example of how neglecting security risks can have a devastating effect on a business comes from a well-known retail pharmacy chain that I was consulting for in 2013. Several years earlier, the company decided to expand its retail network by taking over cheap independent pharmacies that failed to achieve expected business results and were facing bankruptcy. One such pharmacy store seemed to be perfect for takeover. It has changed ownerships four times over a period of less than four years and was experiencing continuous losses which made it cheap. It was also located in a high density residential neighborhood, close to a hospital, and it was the only pharmacy in the area. The Pharmaceutical Company thoroughly assessed the potential benefits and previous flaws and decided to purchase the store. Its strategy was to move one of its best retail store managers to this pharmacy, improve the design of the store, increase its assortment, lower the prices, extend opening hours, and heavily invest in marketing. However, soon after takeover it became clear that previous failures had very little to do with the quality of management and sales tactics. The main reasons were frequent (almost weekly) and costly security incidents such as robberies, thefts, and vandalism which impacted the store directly, but also indirectly as they discouraged potential customers. Moreover, the loss was even more significant because of the higher investment that the company felt was necessary in order to improve the flaws that it had identified. Less than six months after opening, the company decided to close that particular store.

OVERALL RISK MANAGEMENT

As we have already said, risks usually come together. For instance, when exploring the possibilities and the risks of entering a new market, we have to take into account an entire battery of factors that accompany each other. We can define Overall Risk as the overall exposure of an entity or a process to unwanted change in its regular operations or as a result of specific actions that it is taking or due to external circumstances. Overall Risk Management would consequently be the joint assessment and management of all the risks that threaten an organization or that could be the result of its actions, in order to provide reasonable assurance regarding the achievement of objectives. Of course, Overall Risk Management requires understanding risk as a complex phenomenon that is composed of numerous factors instead of assessing and addressing each risk separately.

> Overall Risk Management would be the joint assessment and management of all the risks that threaten an organization.

Overall Risk Management can be either a distinct function that, based on the Overall Risk Matrix, collects inputs from all the other functions, or a Committee that is composed of all the functions that manage specific aspects of risk, whether its effects are direct or indirect. In order to count our overall exposure to risk, we have to take into account all the aspects of our operations or a process, count the influence that each aspects would have on the entire process, assess all the resources and functions that are required to address risks and quantify the total cost of mitigating those risks, as well as the financial consequences of the failure to address them.

We can divide overall risk into four categories:

- Security and Safety Risks
- Direct Financial Risks
- Operational Risk
- Strategic Risk

Security and Safety Risks

Security and Safety Risks can be simply defined as the likelihood of man-made Security and Safety incidents and Natural Catastrophes and the severity of their impact on people, property, and processes.

Direct Financial Risks

This category consists of all the risks that accompany an investment or that can have direct negative influences on value or profit, such as Liquidity risk, Pricing Risk, Asset Devaluation Risk, Foreign Currency Exchange Risk, Credit Risk, etc.

Operational Risk

Operational Risks include all the risks steaming from company's processes, its people, and assets. They, for instance, include Infrastructure failures as a result of inadequate care or due to external events, lack of expertise resulting from knowledge drain, shaken customer satisfaction, unprofitability of the product or service, various integrity related risks, reputational risks, etc.

Strategic Risks

Strategies risk encompasses all the possible sources of loss that might arise from a poor business plan, failure to execute a good strategy, major oversight in assessing risk, and external events that could impact company's strategic operations. Strategic risks include Market Risk, Competition, Trends related to social and cultural values, Availability of Capital, and so forth.

Still, by strictly dividing risks, we miss the opportunity to understand that each group of risks actually contains a blend of other risk groups. For example, security risks impact operational risks, cause direct financial losses, and add to strategic risks.

Risk Management Frameworks

Since recently, many companies are starting to understand the complexity of risk management and are adopting risk management frameworks and standards that do attempt to address risks as a companywide phenomenon, such as Enterprise Risk Management (ERM). ERM is a framework that combines processes and methods of integrating risk controls in a company in order to ensure that they are appropriately managed. Still, as much as these risk management models are indeed a step in a good direction, they are sometimes too complicated, bulky, and too elitist to be practical and effective. Also, risk certainly deserves extra effort. Apart from adopting Frameworks, there are principles that we could additionally use to practically improve our risk management practices which would not be in contradiction with the standards that we are working by, nor with the frameworks that we have adopted.

> Many risk management frameworks tend to be too complicated, bulky and too elitist to be effective.

Risk Mapping

By simply graphically mapping risks by, for instance, using a Spaghetti Chart, we will be able to see the interconnectedness of Risks to understand the scope of functions and actions that are required to address the risk as a whole. Moreover, we will be able to see how security risks contribute to the overall risk profile of a company and its processes. In general, each function needs to have a detailed catalog of assets and processes, to have identified and listed all the probable risks that are associated with them, as well as to understand the role of other functions in addressing those risks. For instance, IT sector will catalog its networks and systems as crucial assets for executing company's key processes. It will further list people, premises, and devices as elements that are necessary for its activities.

Consequently, IT security will assess the risks of data loss and unavailability while security will determine the probability of harmful scenarios that could cause the loss or physical damage to devices. Subsequently, HR will assess the risks related to workforce, such as the local unavailability of expertise, knowledge drain, and employment frauds, but also list security as support in its pre-employment procedures that are part of their strategy to minimize risks. Certainly, all these factors should be included in the overall risk calculation of a process where the activity is performed and the cost of mitigating those risks. For example, when we would assess the risks of entering a new market where we would also want to use our ICT system as part of reaching our objectives in that market, we would have to include the likelihood and severity of events and circumstances that could influence it. These influences would certainly also have to include crime, natural disasters, availability of infrastructure, issues concerning the quality of workforce, etc. Of course, we would include the severity of risks and the cost of overcoming them in our feasibility study and profitability estimations.

> Each function should have a detailed catalogue of risks that it is responsible for and understand the role of other functions in addressing those risks.

Spaghetti Chart

Spaghetti Charts (or diagrams) are mostly used to visually present a process flow in order to determine the efficiency of a process and eliminate wasteful and time consuming activities. However, a Spaghetti Chart can also be extremely useful in Risk Management as a tool that will help us to graphically present all the elements that a process is composed of, and understand their interconnectedness that would afterward be used as part of the Overall Risk Matrix.

Overall Risk Matrix

Basically, the Overall Risk Matrix works like a puzzle. When a project is introduced, each unit whose processes are initially included in the process map will bring along its matrix that illustrates the risks that are associated with its part of the processes, thus contributing to the overall risk profile of the project. Certainly, this approach would result in eventually involving more functions in the project, but also in being more accurate in understanding all the required resources, accompanying risks and total costs, and managing them more effectively and efficiently.

CHAPTER SUMMARY

We are all familiar with the term "micro-management," and often use it to describe ineffective managers. The actual definition of micro-management would be exaggeration in the level of control, concerning both the level of tasks and frequency of control. We will theoretically always choose macro-management over micro-management as we want to reach an objective and not get stuck in small details along the way. Still, macro-managers are often less successful in terms of actual accomplishments. Many organizations prefer to have micro-managers on the lower end of the management hierarchy scale and macro-managers that are designing strategies and managing entire concepts on the top. When it comes to managing processes, we need to be able to control them down to smallest details and still be able to see the wider picture in terms of their influence and interconnectedness and manage them together as an overall concept. Risk is certainly an overall concept and one that is absolutely crucial for the business. It requires both a detailed and strategic approach. Effective risk management requires that we understand and remember the overall objective. It calls for expanding narrow definitions, widening the scope of interest, changing the way in which we assess risks, measure their influence and count potential costs and losses, and being proactive in addressing them.

SELF-ASSESSMENT/DISCUSSION QUESTIONS

1. Do you believe that your company's risk management efforts are comprehensive and effective?
2. In your organization, is there a function or comity that unites all the risk management functions and gathers and analyzes their risk inputs as well as inputs from other functions?
3. Does your organization tend to neglect important risks that are not associated with large investments?
4. Did you clearly define the risk management responsibilities of functions that are not namely risk management functions?
5. Do you have a comprehensive risk management chart that shows the involvement and overlapping of various functions in identifying and addressing risks?

CHAPTER 5

Incident Economics:
Understanding and Quantifying Loss

INTRODUCTION

According to the cost and benefit principle, the investment in security should not exceed the cost of incidents over a reasonable period of time. However, we usually only count the immediate tangible loss and not the overall one. Probably one of the main factors that negatively influence the position of security in companies is the inability of businesses to determine the actual influence of security incidents and think beyond the primary visible loss in order to count the real cost and benefit ratio. By failing to understand impacts, we also weaken our resilience by not anticipating issues, not managing to sufficiently prepare for troubles and properly react to incidents, and finally, making it harder for ourselves to recover from disasters and learn lessons. Moreover, we often even link consequences of certain events to unrelated causes and naturally implement wrong remedies. We actually base important business decisions on information that we have, whether this information is correct or not. We also naturally determine priorities based on importance. Being able to correctly anticipate and evaluate incident, quantify their impact, fully recover, and target the real causes when implementing improvements is absolutely crucial for any business.

> Businesses find it difficult to determine the real influence of security incidents on the business and understand the benefits of investing in security.

THE RISK OF SIMPLIFYING TERMS

The commercial mindset in the quick-win culture pushes us to the direction of simplifying key terms and synonyms and understanding them as immediate categories. When we say success we actually mean instant profit; when we count value, we actually count direct income; when we think of incidents, we think of instant loss. Unfortunately, this simplification of terms causes that we neglect important particulars that have value or could add value and

57

From Corporate Security to Commercial Force. DOI: http://dx.doi.org/10.1016/B978-0-12-805149-8.00005-4

would eventually lead to profit or loss. Moreover, it prevents us from understanding the real extent of gain and loss and not only the immediate visible one that is often even less significant. Both profit and loss are actually the final outcomes of chain reactions. For example, the success of increased reputation will eventually lead to profit. In the same way, loss is not a synonym for incident. Loss is actually the final outcome of the domino effect that started with an incident.

> We equalize success and instant profit, count value through direct income and classify incidents according to immediate losses.

THE CONCEPT OF VALUE

Different Perceptions of Value

In business, we are so accustomed to using the term "Value" that we do not feel the need to further analyze it and explain it. However, one of the biggest reasons why we miscalculate the effects of incidents and fail to fully understand the benefits of security is because we misunderstand the concept of value. Actually, value is a term that can be understood in many different, even opposing, ways. For instance, for a consumer, value is the proportion between the perceived performance or quality of a product or service and its cost. Similarly, in marketing, value is the ratio between customer's assessment of benefits and price. For a business, value is basically the direct profit that it receives from a product or service. Finally, security understands value solely as a motive to commit a crime and in terms of the justified cost of security measures that are used to protect it. Basically, for security, value determines the probability of the element (process, product, person, etc.) being a motive for an action against it. Actually, in some cases, the value can be higher for the enemy than for the business or its loss can even have absolutely no direct financial impact on the business. For instance, toxic waste, such as nuclear waste, has no value for the business. Actually, it even has a negative value in terms of resources required to properly store it or dispose of. However, for a terrorist this waste could be extremely valuable. A cigarette manufacturer will have to spend resources to store and dispose of faulty products that cannot be recycled which has a negative value for the business. Still, faulty stolen products could appear on the black market and severely damage the reputation of the company. The same goes for stolen outdated data that we no longer require but their exposure can still pose a significant risk.

Further, as for different perceptions of value, we can take the example of tin cans that are being manufactured for a soft drink factory. The manufacturer will assess the value according to the profit that it receives from the product.

On the other hand, marketing will only calculate the value of the design of tin cans in terms of how it will raise the perceived value of the final product and convince the customers that the ratio between benefits and price is favorable enough for them to buy it. Finally, security will see no value in the product, simply because it would not perceive it as a good enough motive for a crime.

Obviously, although customers and various business functions understand the concept of value in different ways, they have one thing in common; they all determine the value of something according to the gain that they receive from it. Security also determines value according to gain although it takes into account the degree of gain that the specific element has for the criminal and not the actual advantage that it has for the business.

> Businesses usually wrongly determine the value of something based on the gain that they receive from it.

Primary and Secondary Value

Furthermore, security divides value into primary and secondary value. Primary value is basically the immediate value of a product. For example, cash, jewelry, alcohol, cigarettes, and branded clothing are primary value products. These items can be used immediately by a criminal or easily be sold. As such, they can be attractive as a motive for opportunity crime by a lone perpetrator, but also for organized crime. Secondary value applies to items that have no usability in their current form: For example, branded shirts are primary value items, whereas the textile used to produce them is a secondary value item. It cannot be used directly by the perpetrator but can be used, for example, by another clothes manufacturer. To be resold, it needs to be in a bigger volume, which requires planning, logistics, and prearrangement with the buyer. This indicates that such crime cannot be carried out by a lone perpetrator, but only by an organized group that is able to organize and perform the action. The classification of value also depends on the volume. Basically, big volumes of primary value become secondary value because executing a theft of big volumes requires planning and logistics. For example, several bottles of wine are primary value, whereas a whole truck of wine is secondary value. Stealing a truckload of wine requires an organization, a buyer, logistics, storage space big enough to contain such a volume, and so forth. The type and volume of the protected value, matched with the level of security measures, also indicate the probability of an action and the modus operandi of perpetrators. For instance, in the example of wine bottles, a lone perpetrator is unlikely to target a well-secured warehouse that contains large volumes of packed wine bottles to steal one or two of them. We call this phenomenon the ratio between effort (or risk) and reward [1].

Counting Value According to Loss

Still, we are all taking the wrong path to understand value, and consequently benefits. Basically, it would actually be more accurate if we were to assess the value of any business element according to loss and not according to gain. Basically, a much better model of determining how valuable something is would be to understand the impact that its sudden disappearance would have on the business instead of only taking into account its directs benefits for the business.

> We would be more accurate if we were to assess the value of any business element according to the disadvantage of losing it and not only according to the benefits of having it.

EXPLAINING INCIDENTS

We usually understand incidents as occurrences that have consequences. However, we usually only assess the direct consequences of incidents and will mostly not classify happenings as incidents unless they caused immediate damages. On the contrary, we sometimes simply understand incidents as unpleasant things that happen. In that way, we completely neglect their effects. Actually, we often classify incidents that did not cause immediate damages as "near misses" or "incidents without consequences." However, I do not believe that there is such a thing as "Incident without consequences" and that it is actually a contradiction of terms. Basically, every incident has consequences whether that are immediate and disastrous or delayed and subtle, or both. Unfortunately, the difference is far from being only linguistic as it actually affects our perception and judgment, and consequently, actions and wallet. We could define incidents as manifestations that cause direct or indirect damages or could have a negative impact on the business. Naturally, when counting incidents and designing strategies that should mitigate them, we must take into account all the incidents and near incidents regardless of their consequences.

> We could define incidents as manifestations that cause direct damages or indirect damages or could have a negative impact on the business.

Security Risks

As we like to think big, we understand incidents as large manifestations that cause great damage. Terrorism, violent property crimes, and large scale frauds will certainly cause the greatest damage during a single incident. However, since recently, security professionals have become aware that continuous small scale crimes, whether internal or external, virtual or physical, sometimes prove to be even costlier than big incidents. Actually, incidents do not even have to happen in our own backyard in order to cause us losses. We all know how terrorist attacks in Tunisia, Egypt, and Turkey affected foreign visits to these countries, including to surrounding countries that were not directly targeted by terrorists, and devastated companies, and even entire industries that depended on tourism.

> Continuous small scale crimes, sometimes prove to be even costlier than big incidents.

We typically categorize security risks as internal or external. However, it is not always easy to draw a clear line between internal and external crimes as, in many cases, corporate investigators stumble upon the involvement of employees during investigations of crimes that were believed to be externally committed. We can further divide risks into two groups: "the risk of doing" and "the risk of not doing." Basically, the "doing" group would consist of risks from intentional acts, whereas the second group would consist of negligence risks. Still, in reality, apart from the need to address both groups of risks, we cannot clearly distinguish between them. For instance, the reputation of an organization could be jeopardized by intentional acts as well as by oversight [2]. Moreover, a bad hire could occur even after we have performed perfect background screening. Actually, the biggest threat for an organization is undoubtedly the combination of both groups—intended incidents that we are not trying to prevent, notice, understand, stop, and recover from. Attempting to provide a complete list of possible security risks would be an impossible mission so I would only mention the most common ones:

- Global or local political and/or economic developments with a potential to alter the security climate
- Crimes against property, such as Embezzlement, Theft, Burglary, Robbery, Frauds, Scams, Vandalism, Sabotage, etc.
- Crimes against person, such as Sexual Harassment, Mobbing, Assault, Workplace violence, etc.
- Cybercrime and High-Tech crimes
- Self-inflected crimes, such as Substance Abuse, Gambling, Self-Mutilation, Suicide, etc.
- Acts of Protests and Strikes
- Terrorism
- Natural Factors

Incidents and Their Impact

On one hand, in business, we know how to correctly define a process as a set of activities and business tasks that will accomplish a goal. Logically, we know that the performance (or underperformance) of each part of the process will influence the final outcome. Basically, businesses are divided into sectors that have their own budgets and cost centers and each sector is responsible for meeting specific objectives and achieving particular results that together make-up a successful business lifecycle. Moreover, each part of the business is responsible for preventing failures and learning from them if they happen anyway. However, sectors will often only assess the negative impact of failures in their own backyard without assessing the impact that these failures will have on the business as a whole. Our understanding of the actual influence and cost of a security incident that occurred in a certain part of a process and its effect on the entire process is unfortunately often very shallow.

> Business sectors will often only asses the negative impact of failures that they are directly responsible for without trying to understand the impact that these failures will have on the entire business.

EXPLAINING LOSS

So, what do we really mean when we characterize loss as being an outcome of a chain reaction that started with an incident? For example, the loss due to a bank robbery does not consist only of the direct loss of stolen cash. Actually, with cash being insured, we are looking in the wrong place. The real loss is the result of service stoppage, closed branch, damages to the morale of the employees, damages to the reputation of the bank, and the "soft target" label that will certainly discourage clients and attract more robbers. On the example of the Supply Chain, an incident could be the theft of raw materials from a transport heading for production. Loss, on the other hand, is the negative outcome of all the events that are linked to that incident and that affect the bottom line, such as cost of stolen goods, production delays, being out of stock on points of sale, and consequently, loss of consumers' confidence, and their switch to a more reliable manufacturer.

> Loss is the final financial outcome of all the events that are linked to an incident.

In the event of a security incident with raw materials that consequently affected sales, it is possible that each sector will separately assess the situation and make wrong conclusions. For example, Production will record a set-back and blame it on the uptime; Logistics will blame the delay on low stock; but still, the main wrongdoers for the loss of profit will appear to be Marketing and Sales and the apparent failure of the marketing strategy and sales efforts. Finally, in order to compensate for the bad business results, the company could paradoxically decide to save costs on security which is usually the first one on the cost saving priority list.

Another threat is issues related to brand integrity, such as loss of imprinted packaging material. So not only that a theft can delay production but can also facilitate counterfeiting. Forged products in the original packaging are certainly a nightmare for every business. We all know that high numbers of forged products on the market impact the reputation of the brand and customer confidence thus causing the drop in sales. Actually, we will assess our losses according to our understanding of value. Business will certainly count the stolen shipment of chocolate wrappers as a hustle but, in terms of financial losses, it would, based on cost, most probably count it as insignificant. Marketing would not take into account any losses as it actually only sees the design as a benefit but does not count its loss as a threat. However, should the wrappers be used for counterfeiting, the actual damages that would be the result of shaken brand reputation and client confidence could be enormous. A good example of the damages is certain well-known cigarette brands that were massively forged and as such sold on the streets of Belgrade, Serbia during the time of international economic sanctions during 1990s. Even after the manufacturers reentered the market, managed to win the battle against criminals, and launched legitimate products, those brands did not manage to regain credibility. After more than 15 years these cigarette brands were still perceived as unreliable by consumers and were eventually removed from the market by manufacturers because they did not produce expected results. We often forget that security plays a big part in business competition. It is one of the key ingredients of business continuity, availability, reliability, accuracy, and reputation which are the business elements that not only count but actually make a difference.

> Security plays a big part in business competition through the assurance of availability, reliability, accuracy and reputation.

INSURANCE AS SECURITY STRATEGY

We usually think of insurance as the magic remedy that will prevent or cure loss. However, insurance often gives as the false sense of security. Weighing the cost of security and the cost of insurance might seem logical. Unfortunately, we sometimes end up canceling our security and choosing insurance instead, as a cheaper alternative. However, insurance does practically nothing to prevent incidents, understand their impact, or reimburse accompanying losses. It actually addresses only one portion of immediate visible losses. Moreover, logically, our insurance fees will grow after every incident. Furthermore, we will be able to protect ourselves only from the financial impact of some of the identified risks but not from all possible risks. That leaves the majority of possible incidents unaddressed and countless possible losses not refunded. Still, insurance is surely useful as part of the mechanism intended to control probable losses and should certainly be part of the overall loss protection strategy of a company.

> Insurance does practically nothing to prevent incidents, understand their impact or reimburse accompanying losses.

INCIDENT COST ANALYSIS

It would be actually very difficult to accurately quantify incidents. Putting a price tag on spoiled reputation, damaged moral, decreased motivation, or for instance damages caused by data leakage would be practically impossible. However, linking events and recognizing the actual depth of incidents would certainly bring us closer to understanding their practical influence and financial implications.

Immediate Loss

When we count the impact of incidents, we often only consider physical damages. In case of a violent armed robbery of a store, we will count the cost of concrete losses, such as the cost of stolen goods and damages to the property. Furthermore, we actually often do not even calculate the selling price of the item but only the amount that we have paid for it. So, to start with, we completely neglect the loss of revenue in the primary loss estimation, or the time and effort that we have invested in maintaining, advertising, and selling the goods. Furthermore, there are incidents that are not accompanied by immediate financial losses, such as sex crimes and mobbing. However, these incidents can turn out to be very costly in terms of legal fees, damaged morale, ruined reputation, etc. As for injuries, we also usually only address physical injuries, including allowing our employees that were physically injured the necessary time to heal and recover. However, the way that you support an employee that was psychologically distressed during an incident would mean more for the moral of the entire organization than most of the HR trainings that are specifically designed to increase the motivation of employees.

> The way that you support an employee that was psychologically distressed during an incident would mean more for the moral of the entire organization than most of the HR trainings.

The Blueprint of Loss

We have already mentioned the effects and costs that incidents in one part of a process can have on the rest of the process. When we talk about the loss of the actual product, we also have to count the illegal sale of our lost product as a loss. Basically, our losses will immediately double as someone will actually buy our stolen goods instead of buying our product that is being sold legitimately. Apart from the double cost of the product we also risk the delay of goods to consumers or even running out of stock at the point of sale. In these cases, not only will criminals profit, so will the competition. Especially in the case of fast-moving consumer goods that do not have a recognizable brand identity, consumers will buy the product that is available at the point of sale at least as a temporary replacement, and will sometimes even turn to another manufacturer permanently. Even when we talk about recognizable brands, globalization has certainly impacted brand loyalty and even minor flaws can turn our customers away from us and send them to the competition. We should not forget that criminals are also competition. Furthermore, the illegal sale of stolen cargo undercuts prices in legitimate businesses. Even retailers will in some cases buy stolen goods from another supplier and order less from us. We must know that as much as we are investigating market potential and working on attracting new consumers, so are the criminals. The fact that our products were stolen means that there is a demand for it on the black market. Of course, like any market, black market expects regular supplies, and the demand grows with each supply. To make it worse, because we were the victim of a successful theft, we have proven to be a soft target and are proving it more with each theft. It is estimated that, on average, one successful incident leads to 10 more incidents against the same target [3]. So, actually attempting to count all the losses that were caused by a seemingly insignificant incident would result in shocking findings. However, we have so far only analyzed direct losses.

Linked Losses

When quantifying the impact of incidents, apart from initial costs, we also need to include the associated costs, such as repeated order, investigation, wasted resources, higher insurance, etc. We have to further assess the likelihood of linked events and delayed consequences or the influence of the event on initiating future similar events, its effect on processes such as our ability to quickly recover and minimize the damage, loss of productivity and morale, damages to our reputation, and finally, profit. Furthermore, in case of excise goods, such as cigarettes and alcohol, the appearance of such products in a market where they should not be sold could result in enormous penalties for the company.

PROCESS MAPPING AND CALCULATION

Companies are increasingly implementing Lean Manufacturing. They are mapping activities that add value and eliminating those that do not add value. However, not many companies actually pay attention to, and address occurrences that take away value. Actually, as much as Lean Manufacturing proved to be a successful business practice in increasing productivity, the reduction of resources to operational minimum also increased the impact of possible incidents. Unfortunately, Lean Manufacturing philosophies do not pay attention to security risks, do not include security in their process mapping, and do not even try to record and analyze security incidents with their metrics. However, security is simply a very important part of the business and it will do much better by applying good business practices. Certainly business will also benefit from letting security in.

> Most business improvement philosophies don't pay attention to security risks, don't include security in their process mapping and don't analyze security incidents with their metrics.

Lean Manufacturing

Lean has two main principles:

- Making the customer satisfied
- Doing it profitably

Both principles actually come down to having the product available when and where it is needed, charging the least possible for it and not compromising on its quality. In Lean, we make sure that we provide quality by using several available business tools. Consequently, we cut the costs by removing activities and costs that do not add value, such as cutting stock and reducing resources to the operational minimum. Logically, because of reduced resources, we invest special efforts in ensuring that our remaining resources work properly so that delivery would not be interrupted. For instance, we want to make sure that our machines are properly maintained to minimize the possibility of failures that could cause production stoppage. We implement special workplace organization methods in order to ensure efficiency and effectiveness. We also pay attention to the safety of employees in order to ensure that we will have the critical number of employees available to produce the product and that we will not have lost working time (Lost Time Injury/LTI) that is caused by injuries. And still, it is rather interesting that the Lean philosophy does not recognize security issues as possible causes as business discontinuity and injury. Although primarily designed as business philosophy that is intended for manufacturing, the general principles of Lean are equally applicable to any type of industry.

Process Mapping

Process Mapping is one of the most important tools of Lean Manufacturing. It maps the value stream by detailing specific actions and resources that compose the entire process from the arrival of raw material required for production up to the arrival of the actual product to consumer. By using various mapping tools, a company can identify various process steps that either add value or cost money.

Lean Security

Lean Security should also use process mapping in order to understand the impact of incidents and quantify losses. Basically, security should use the map of processes and resources and use it to list probable incidents for each part of the process and the impact that these incidents could have on all the elements of the process, such as resources, time, people, delivery, etc. It should be able to understand the operational and financial impact that one incident has on the part of the process where it occurred, on all the following stages of the processes and consequently, on the final product and the consumer, and count the overall loss. Still, the precondition for that would be that security has the ability to monitor processes and that it is integral part of the Lean Process. Unfortunately, in most cases, security is placed in one sector of the company, for instance in Operations, based simply on accounting convenience, which practically prevents it from overseeing the entire Value Stream. Moreover, security is typically unjustly excluded from most modern business improvement philosophies and practices.

> Security should use process mapping in order to understand the impact of incidents on the entire business and accurately quantify losses.

CHAPTER SUMMARY

Linking security to the business and running it like a core business process would produce numerous benefits for a company. By including this missing link to the maps of our core processes, we will make a big step toward noticing harmful events that affect processes, take away value, and cost money. Certainly, comprehending causes and realizing their influences is the precondition for any improvement, crucial element of effective risk management of any commercial entity, and the fundament of its overall resilience. However, this actually requires that security is practically given the mandate, support, and opportunity to assess core business processes, be included in them and participate in business decisions. It also takes upgrading, adapting, and widening the scope of our business philosophies and practices so that they would be able to completely include security in business operations and directions.

SELF-ASSESSMENT/DISCUSSION QUESTIONS

1. Does your organization collect data and analyses near misses and incidents that did not result in visible consequences?
2. Does your organization have the mechanisms to understand how security incident that occurred in one part of a process affect the entire process and the company?
3. Do you attempt to count all the direct and indirect losses that result from incidents?
4. Do you believe that insurance and legal instruments have the capacity to prevent most losses?
5. Do you regard and treat psychological distress following an incident at work in the same way that you treat work-related physical injury?
6. Do you invest efforts in analyzing how business optimization models that you are implementing may affect security and resilience of the company and parallelly address these issues?

References

[1] M. Cabric, Corporate Security Management. Challenges, Risks, and Strategies, Butterworth-Heinemann, Oxford, 2015, p. 5.

[2] M. Cabric, Corporate Security Management. Challenges, Risks, and Strategies, Butterworth-Heinemann, Oxford, 2015, p. 89.

[3] M. Cabric, Corporate Security Management. Challenges, Risks, and Strategies, Butterworth-Heinemann, Oxford, 2015, p. 151.

CHAPTER 6

Quantifying Information Security: *Calculating the Intangible*

THE CHALLENGES OF MEASURING

It has become clear that lack of investment in Information Security is as guilty for security failures as lack of skill. Moreover, it is investment that also influences skill. Basically, in theory, the more we pay, the more value we receive in return, both in terms of technology and in terms of professional expertise. And still, both funding and knowledge prove to be completely useless without the third comprehensive element that unites the other two in producing actual results—care. Out of the three elements, it is exactly care that usually makes the difference between a good performance and a failure. In commercial organizations, especially those that do invest in security systems, one of the frequent obstacles is a phenomenon that economists refer to as Moral Hazard, or simply the "we shouldn't worry, it's been paid for" attitude. Unfortunately, the even more frequent difficulty is the opinion of decision makers that security is nothing more than a cost and a hustle, as presenting the benefits of security to stakeholders rarely involves explaining competitive advantage and how it relates to profit, probably as accurately measuring the actual benefits poses a serious challenge.

Businesses base their strategies on facts or at least on educated guesses. They find it hard to manage risks without knowing their impact and the benefits and understanding if they pay too much, too little, or just enough to protect from risks. To add to the complexity, risks and vulnerabilities constantly oscillate, both in terms of severity and frequency. Naturally, the value of information security oscillates as well. Basically, in order to be accurate in measuring, we have to continuously reevaluate the risks and the benefits and assess vulnerabilities which is not as nearly as simple a task as it may seem. Moreover, any type of risk management activity should be detailed and at the same time simple enough to explain risks to top management. Of course, considering the sophistication of information security risks and what is at stake, being able to efficiently explain the risks to stakeholders, raise their

From Corporate Security to Commercial Force. DOI: http://dx.doi.org/10.1016/B978-0-12-805149-8.00006-6

awareness, and receive their support are some of the most challenging parts of security manager's job description.

> Every risk management activity should be detailed in approach and simple in explanation.

Still, for businesses, quantifying any processes is very important as the ability to measure gives them the idea of its importance, allows them to control it, optimize it, and invest the proper amount of attention, skill, and funds in managing it and protecting it. Actually, it is definitely an imperative to be able to quantify something as important as Security. However, while it seems achievable to relatively accurately quantify physical security by measuring security incidents that might occur in a commercial organization, anticipating their frequency, and severity and determining their direct and indirect influence on the business, and consequently counting their cost, quantifying Information and ICT Security often seems like an impossible mission.

THE VALUE OF INFORMATION SECURITY

When counting the value of Information Security for a business, the first questions that we ask ourselves are whether investments in information security add value to the company and if security improvements actually create bottom-line business benefits. Simply put, is a secure organization more valuable than an insecure one? Naturally, we cannot count the value of information security as a standalone system but according to the value that it is tasked to safeguard and its importance for the business, measured against probable defects that this value may be endangered by and their severity and impact.

ICT has become the fifth key department of a business, together with other four traditional departments—Operations, Sales, Finances, and Human Resources. Moreover, the importance of the role that ICT has for a business is growing daily. The currently trending topic for most companies is digital transformation and how to face the business with new technologies. ICT is not only a department but the infrastructure and a service that can be compared to the role that bloodstream has for the human organism. However, when assessing the value of Information Security, we cannot determine it according to our investment in the ICT department and its financial value, but on the real importance that the ICT infrastructure has for the business. Basically, Information Security does not only protect the ICT infrastructure and information that it contains, but we can even look at it as a parallel universe where almost every physical element of the business lives virtually. However, every change in the virtual world reflects on the physical one.

> ICT can be compared to the role that bloodstream has for the human organism.

Determining the Purpose and Importance of Services

We could summarize Information Security as all the efforts of an organizations aimed at protecting its information from unauthorized access, use, disclosure, disruption, modification, or destruction. Determining the value of Information Security as a whole would be practically impossible without dividing it according to principles that it is tasked to protect and analyzing the importance of feature for the business.

CIA Triad

The basic aims of information security are often summarized in three principles called the CIA triad which stands for confidentiality, integrity, and availability. It has been argued that CIA triad does not address all the principles of information security and that some other principles should be added, such as Possession, Authenticity, and Utility. However, CIA triad is still the fundamental concept in Information Security and the first step in designing any secure system. Confidentiality means making sure that information is accessible only to people who have the right to see it. Integrity requires ensuring that information remains intact and unaltered. Availability implies that people who have the right to access information can have access to it and be able to use it when they need it. Basically, Availability means that nothing should be able to block legitimate and timely access to information and systems. Naturally, for each of the principles, we use different measures.

Confidentiality requires Access Control that consists of procedures and measures aimed at controlling physical and technical access to information and systems. We use digital signatures and similar protocols to ensure Integrity, that information remains intact and unaltered and to preserve its integrity. The role of Business Continuity Management and Disaster Recovery is to make sure that our systems, services, and information remain available, or become available shortly after an incident. Naturally, our information and systems have value for us only if we can access them and use them in our business processes. The proportion in which companies address Confidentiality, Integrity, and Availability differs from industry to industry and from organization to organization, mostly according to their specific needs and requirements, use of ICT systems and networks, and the importance of each of the principles for the business. For instance, an industrial facility will focus on availability of the ICT systems that support production. Law office and medical institution will invest most of their efforts in ensuring the integrity and confidentiality of data. A bank will naturally equally focus on all three aspects in order to stop unauthorized access, prevent any type of fraud, and ensure that its systems are available and working properly.

> Our information and systems have value only if we can access them and use them in our business processes.

THE DIFFERENCE BETWEEN PHYSICAL AND INFORMATION SECURITY

Integrity

One of the main differences between physical security and information security is certainly the nature of the protected asset. For instance, in physical security, when an item is lost, it is immediately written-off. Our loss will be the same regardless of what a criminal does with our stolen asset. For instance, if a chocolate has been stolen from retail, the supermarket could not care less if the criminal will eat it, sell it, or throw it away. In case of stolen (copied) information, the extent of damage actually depends on what a criminal does with it, as information has no monetary value unless it is being used. Naturally, when we measure the integrity part of physical security, we can relatively accurately quantify it. On the other hand, in order to quantify integrity in information security, we have to measure the consequences of the worst-case scenario as we are not able to control what will happen with the asset after it was stolen. As we cannot control what will happen with information after it was stolen, we assume that the outcome will be catastrophic.

> In case of stolen information, the extent of damage depends on what a criminal does with it.

As for the model in which we protect assets, if we talk about physical security, the number of exits through which a physical asset can exit the facility is limited. Basically, whether the theft is committed internally or externally, the perpetrators will have a limited number of places where they can enter the facility and exit it with stolen goods. In case of information security, anyone that has access, or is able to gain access, to networks and systems is a potential exit point.

Confidentiality

Naturally, our protection of the physical asset stopes the moment it was stolen. On the other hand, in Information security we continue to protect the asset also after it was stolen in order to prevent anyone unauthorized from being able to use stolen information. In physical security we basically use the wrapper to protect the chocolate until it reaches the consumer. In information security, we want to make sure that the wrapper will protect the chocolate until it reaches the end user but at the same time prevent an unauthorized user from opening it and consuming it.

> We continue to protect the information also after it was stolen.

Availability

Availability addresses the aspect of service stoppage. In industrial enterprises, unavailability implies that a company would not be able to continue its core business processes such as production and sales. However, as customers are not part of the process, discontinuity will affect the company and not the client. For instance, as a result of unavailability of key systems, a shoe manufacturer would not be able to continue manufacturing the shoes or selling them online through their website. Still, depending on the severity of service stoppage, the customers will still be able to buy the products that are in stock, or available in retail. If the issue would not be resolved for a longer time, the customers will acquire the product from the competition. While the company would encounter losses, the disruption would not necessarily impact its reputation nor its clients. When it comes to the industries of financial or telecommunication services, unavailability could, depending on the nature of the disrupting event, immediately impact the client. Actually, the more important our client is, the more he/she will be impacted by disruptions. While for production enterprises, ensuring availability is the most important aspect of Information Security, Business Continuity, and Disaster Recovery is still more important and more valued in the industry of financial services. For instance, it is rare that industrial enterprises have disaster recovery sites that are located away from the original business site and contain duplicated, independently hosted crucial ICT systems that can provide normal business operations in case of a disaster. For financial institutions, disaster recovery sites have become a standard. Disaster Recovery sites are also officially standardized in ISO 22301 which includes both Physical and Logical security approaches to Business Continuity and Disaster Recovery.

MEASURING INFORMATION SECURITY ACCORDING TO THREATS

Threats and Risks

First of all, we should clear out the mix-up between Threat and Risk. Although there has always been a confusion about the difference between these two terms, even amongst security professionals that use and work with both terms daily, the difference is actually quite clear. Simply put, "threat" is the intent of the enemy or the potential of Force Majeure to cause harm, whereas "risk" is a threat that can actually cause harm, usually as result of a failure to properly identify and address vulnerabilities. Basically, threats will always exist but it is our task to identify them and implement strategies that will minimize the actual risks.

Risk is a threat that has the potential to cause harm, usually as result of a failure to properly identify and address vulnerabilities.

A friend of mine, Javier Espinosa, likes to use the example of a goldfish bowl to explain the difference between Threat, Risk, and Vulnerability. If a goldfish bowl is cracked, the crack is vulnerability, the water inside the bowl is threat while actual risks depend on our assets, and can include the death of the goldfish and flooded carpet [Javier Espinosa, personal communication, October 20, 2016].

Threats Change

Protection costs money and that money has to be justified. Second, protection changes as threats change. The threats that were relevant yesterday might not be relevant tomorrow. Therefore, protection that was good in the past might not be good enough in the future. Also, as much as we would want protection to change as fast as threats change, the reality is different. As much as regular risk assessments can help identify new threats, our measures still must hold water for a reasonable period. Simply put, we want to make sure that the potential cost of no security would be higher than our investment in it, as well as that our spending would protect us from the risks for a relatively long time. Of course, the key word that we have to use when talking about protection is "relative," as we know both from theory and from our practical experience, that there is no absolute security. Naturally, the higher the level of imperfection of our systems, the higher the probability of incidents. However, there are no two relatively secured companies that have the identical level of security and that have implemented identical measures against threats.

We want to make sure that the potential cost of no security would be higher than our investment in it, and that this investment would protect us from the risks for a relatively long time,

Absolute Metrics

Absolute metrics are metrics that involve quantitative measures that are not relative to, or dependent on anything else and basically tell us that we can measure all the organizations by using the same criteria. We can explain absolute metrics on the example of watering a plant. For instance, according to the principle of absolute metrics we will give two different plants the same amount of water at the same time of the day, and expect their growth to be identical in terms of both speed and height. Actually, explaining and defending strategies by using absolute metrics is almost impossible as we can only talk about the "what" element of a strategy and not its "why" counterpart which is actually the reason why we use a certain strategy in the first place. Basically, we can be accurate in explaining how much water we use to water a plant but not why we do it. Some security experts argue that there could be no absolute metrics when we talk about security. To start with, every organization is different in terms of industry, processes, size, product, and agenda, just to mention a few. On top of that, all organizations, even similar ones, uniquely interpret the terms "secure" and "insecure" and consequently uniquely conceptualize protection, both in terms of strategies, the level that they want to reach and the amount of risk that they are willing to accept. On the other hand, even very similar organizations with almost identical protection setups sometimes experience a very different frequency, severity, and impacts of incidents. For example, two restaurants might use the same meat vendor and prepare a steak according to the identical recipe, and still, as the meat comes from different heifers and requires a different treatment, the outcome will eventually be different.

Security Concept and Business Context

What everyone seems to agree on is that, when measuring efforts against the dangers, we actually want to reach the situation when the ratio between threats and measures, as well as that of reasonable costs of measures and the cost of probable flaws, would be favorable for the company. Naturally, that would be impossible unless security is part of company strategy. Security is obviously not a concept that exists without a context and does not have a meaning without adding "of" and "from" to it—"security of…" and "protection from…." While the "security of" aspect depends on us, and is as such to some extent easier to comprehend, the "protection from" part depends on external factors and is certainly more difficult to assess. Logically, in our efforts to quantify security, it is especially the factors that we do not control that deserve our outmost attention.

> Security is a concept that exists within a context and requires adding "of" and "from" to it

Sufficient Security

We often use the term "Sufficient Security" to explain the relatively good level of security that is based on the ratio between threats and their potential impact, measures against these threats, and the cost of measures. Basically, "sufficient" means that we will just implement measures that will provide reasonable protection. However, as we have said, threats change and arranging security in a way that it just barely addresses them puts us at risks. If our security measures only address threats and vulnerabilities, we will base it on the identified threats as it would be almost impossible to predict future ones. So, it seems that completely relying only on the threats would not be sufficient for protecting from them. Moreover, by labeling measures as sufficient we not only risk Moral Hazard but also make the approval of any proximate further investments in security very unlikely. We can compare sufficient security with building a dam to provide sufficient protection based on the current level of the river although we know that water levels will continuously raise in the future.

IDENTIFYING INFORMATION SECURITY THREATS

Identifying Threats

We did identify that threats shape our strategies and although we might not be able to efficiently quantify them, we should do our best to identify them and anticipate them. While at first glance, this might seem like an impossible mission, there are ways to foresee the threats. To some extent, although many organizations believe that the threats that they are facing are unique, the truth is that most threats are common to most organizations, especially the ones that belong to the same industry. Therefore, time and efforts, and even money that are invested in learning about common threats would not be wasted. However, that certainly does not mean that unidentified and unanticipated risks should not receive their share of attention. Collecting the data about incidents will also help us to establish threat patterns. When we talk about incidents, apart from analyzing all the incidents and their consequences regardless if they occurred in our organization or in a similar organization, we should not forget to collect the data and analyze near-misses—the incidents that had the potential to cause damages but did not. Finally, we should not forget about instincts and not be afraid to occasionally make an investment in information security based on a hunch on top of our reason based strategies. We will make a big step toward the early identification of threats by joining forums, networking, investing efforts in gathering and processing information, and contracting consulting companies that are able to collect and analyze relevant data. However, it depends on the agility of the company if the time period between a new threat has emerged, and until it was identified by the company and addressed with actual measures, would be acceptable or not.

> Most information security threats are common to most organizations, especially the ones belonging to the same industry.

Incident Statistics

To really understand the extent of risk and damage, and basically come to the conclusion that there are no organizations that are completely protected from data breach and that the consequences can indeed be catastrophic, we can look at some official statistics that summarize year 2015. Here we have to divide the threats by those that are the result of "doing" (actions against us) and the ones that are the result of "not doing" (not doing enough to protect from threats). Based on the "ITRC Data Breach Reports—2015 Year-End Totals" report [1], over 169 million personal records were exposed as a result of 781 publicized data breaches in 2015. Further, according to IBM/ Ponemon [2], the average cost of each stolen record was US$ 154, while in healthcare the average cost is US$ 363 per record. Price Waterhouse Coopers (PWC) states in its "The Global State of Information Security Survey 2016" report [3] that there were 38% more incidents in 2015 compared to the year before. According to Microsoft Advanced Threat Analytics [4] the average time that attackers stay dormant within a network before being detected is over 200 days. As for the risks of "not doing," based on the ISACA International report "2015 Global Cybersecurity Status Report" [5], only 38% of global organizations claim that they are prepared for sophisticated cyberattacks. On top of that, the "2015 Trustwave Global Security Report" [6] reveals that 81% of data breach victims that were surveyed report that they had neither a system nor in-house service that could detect data breaches and completely relied on notifications from external parties. However, this is only the tip of the iceberg which does not come even close to analyzing all the threats that Information Security should prevent, including, but not limited to business continuity issues that are the result of natural catastrophes.

Internal Risks

We often simplify when it comes to risks and divide risks according to external ones that we know that we do not control, and internal ones that we think that we control. That is the main reason why some businesses tend to neglect the internal factors when assessing risks. Actually, many times it is the employees that are guilty for compromising information, whether accidentally or intentionally. Even when we do restrict access to information to those who need it, information may leak as a result of human error. We can even say that it is many times the desire of employees to complete their tasks and work overload that are the reason that they would copy databases and send them by email so that they could continue working at home. Moreover, information is not always compromised by purely electronic means. Many, even most, employees print out confidential information so that they could continue working on it. It is not rare that confidential document end up being openly displayed on the back seat of a car or thrown in a public trash can. We should also not forget stolen laptops, smartphones, and memory sticks. As for malicious insiders, their actions are usually the result of dissatisfaction with the company or its employees, industrial espionage or intent to sell information on the black market. Naturally, internal risks are not limited only to copying information but also to erasing and altering. Insiders are actually quite an enigma for many commercial organizations and often not properly addressed, usually because of the lack of awareness, but also due to restrictions imposed by the laws relating to trade unions.

> We divide risks according to external ones that we know that we don't control, and internal ones that we think that we control.

Case Study: Confidential Customer Data

In autumn 2012, one of the Vice President and some top executives from the headquarters of a bank that I was working for payed a visit to one of the markets where the bank had been operating. After a very satisfactory meeting with the local CEO, the visitors went sightseeing and decided to try out some local street food. They ended-up buying roasted chestnuts from a street vendor that was located in the vicinity of bank's local head office. The chestnuts were however rapped in documents that are belonging to the bank that contained very sensitive customer information. As the following investigation revealed, the documents were accidently thrown to a garbage container nearby the day before.

COST—BENEFIT ANALYSIS OF INFORMATION SECURITY

As we have said earlier, being able to accurately determine security costs is a prerequisite for any cost—benefit calculation. However, even when we identify the costs, we still do not know the correct formula for counting the portion of the budget that should be spent on security and if what we spend will be enough to protect us from the risks. Furthermore, in order to measure the benefits of information security, we have to know the cost of damages that would occur if we did not have security measures and compare it to the cost of measure that we are implementing and how these measures will lower the cost of damages. We can relatively accurately count how much we spend on Information Security by counting the costs of information security incidents, the costs of managing information security, the costs of implemented measures, and regulatory costs. Still, by counting these four aspects of Information Security costs, we will only be able to understand how much we have spent on information security which will still tell us nothing about the actual benefits and if what we spend is sufficient to protect us from risks.

Regulatory Costs

Apart from cost of measures that we want to implement, we cannot forget the cost of measures that we have to implement. The amount and frequency of security and privacy regulations that are being imposed by regulators and therefore also their costs are continuously growing. One of the threats that involves regulatory costs that affects many companies is not matching actual needs with imposed regulations which results in the overlapping of measures and spending double on addressing a single issue. One of the main reasons is usually the centralized model of governance by which a company imposes strict rules that all parts of the business have to obey, without adjusting these rules to local regulations or allowing remote parts of the business to do that by only supplying them with standards instead of turnkey policies. On the operational side, many companies get lost in fulfilling regulatory requirements in a way that they focus completely shifts from security objectives to compliance.

> Many companies get lost in fulfilling regulatory requirements in a way that they completely focus on compliance instead of on reaching security objectives.

Budgeting Formula

Many analysts continuously work on finding the right formula that would show what percentage of the budget should be spent of information security. Naturally, we should forget about trying to come-up with any budgeting formula simply because our budget has nothing to do with the risks and they cannot be put into a proportion. The most that we could come-up with is the average percentage of the budget that commercial organizations in general spend on Information Security which could be a completely wrong formula when applied to our circumstances. Still, according to the industry and sector, we can find different benchmarking groups where metrics are shared. Such sanitized data can certainly be of help.

> Our budget and the risks that we are facing cannot be put into a proportion.

QUANTIFYING CONFIDENTIALITY, INTEGRITY, AND AVAILABILITY

Quantifying Availability

To measure Availability is quite simple and we do it regularly and quite accurately by using Business Impact Analysis (BIA). The main objectives of BIA are to identify critical processes and the impact (operational, economic, reputational, etc.) on the company if these processes stop. A good BIA will relatively precisely measure the impact of unavailability on business operations and determine how lost time affects the impact. With BIA, we will also be able to determine what are the crucial systems that we need and relatively accurately count how much we should invest in ensuring business continuity and disaster recovery of these systems. Basically, whatever we want to invest in our Business Continuity and Disaster Recovery, including investing in a disaster recovery site with duplicated, independently hosted systems, it is easily quantifiable and justifiable.

Attempts to Quantify Confidentiality and Integrity

Unlike measuring the importance of Availability, quantifying the effects of Confidentiality and Integrity flaws is not as nearly as simple. A successful model for measuring Confidentiality and Integrity has not yet been invented, and I doubt that it will be invented soon. One of the attempts to measure the impact of Confidentiality and Integrity flaws is by counting the impact that these flaws would have on the reputation of the company and equalizing the effects of damaged reputation due to information security flaws with the effects of bad customer service. As example, for a bank preserving the confidentiality and integrity of their clients' data is an important part of its customer service. Consequently, breaching that confidence would mean risking that its clients take their business elsewhere. This, we would actually be able to measure if we use statistical data that will tell us the average percentage of customers that are likely to change the bank due to bad customer service. However, we would still not able to know how many clients would be affected by a potential breach, before it actually happens (and sometimes not even then) and whether clients would react in the same way to generally bad customer service and severe privacy issues. Basically, consumers' decisions do not rely only on customer service but on numerous other aspects, such as convenience, price, marketing, brand, etc. Moreover, we still did not count law suits, actual damages, direct and indirect losses, and cost of repair, not to mention the loss of intellectual property. Also, this model relies on customer data but completely ignores the possibility that there could be no customers involved and that the threat would actually be that our own expensive data gets stolen. It is actually often more difficult to put a price tag on our data than on customer data. Finally, this model of measuring only attempts to quantify incidents but not the concrete value of Integrity and Availability.

MANAGING INFORMATION SECURITY

Managing information security is an ongoing process that is, just like physical security management, based on the seven essential pillars: all the horizontal and vertical levels of people, physical aspects of data, multiple layers of technology, smart governance, ability to effectively collect and process Information, effective communication between all those that are concerned with security, and professional management that is able to analyze, design, implement, and control. This basically means understanding and managing information security as the core element of the culture of an organization.

However, there are certain conditions that would enable it. The Chief Information Security Officer (CISO) must be able to present frequently to the board of directors. Also, while Information Security functions continuously move from operational activities to policy and governance, they also have to continue to perform hands-on activities. Many CISOs report to the ICT function which not only creates a conflict of interest and prevents the CISO from efficiently controlling the ICT department, but also has limited influence on the business management which makes the investment of the proper amount of funds and attention in Information Security very unlikely. Last but certainly not least, technology is important but it is the people that make a difference. Skilled labor is the greatest resource used in information security. A good system requires skilled and dedicated in-house staff that manage the majority of tasks while delegating only some responsibilities to external service providers. And still, outsourcing of ICT security services is continuously increasing due to efficiency programs while skilled and trusted resources are increasingly difficult to get.

> Skilled labor is the greatest resource used in information security.

HOW MUCH SHOULD WE ACTUALLY PAY?

It would be nice to always be able to determine the percentage of risk that a security incident will affect our organization, accurately assess the impact that the incident may have, and invest just the right amount of money in preventing it. Unfortunately, that will not happen. Information risk should be thought of as an uncertainty. Consequently, we should manage uncertainty by using probability to lower probability. Going back to the beginning of the chapter—the more we pay, the more we will get in return. On top of that, something as important as Information Security deserves that we invest in it as much as we can in order to close as many identified gaps and protect from as many identified risks as we can. Actually, the only risk of paying a lot for information security is that we will have less money left. On the other hand, we would certainly always risk to lose a lot more by not investing. Also, there is no risk of paying too much when it comes to performance. First of all, our security cannot be too good, just better. Second, if we carefully manage all the aspects of security, there is no reason why our spending will exceed the benefits that we receive in return. As we can really forget about trying to quantify our data and the threats that it faces, we should stop attempting to come-up with the right formula for investing in information security that is based on these elements. Simply, our Information Security budgeting formula should be based on our financial abilities to address threats. Fundamentally, we should spend on it as much as we can so that it is not painful. We should further allocate the funds according to the importance that a certain feature of Information Security has for the organization and the cost of protecting these features. Logically, even if our first priority would be Integrity, the reasonable level of integrity still might be cheaper than the reasonable level of Business Continuity Management and Disaster Recovery which, to start with, calls for more investment. Finally, be understanding Information Security as a function and not as an overall effort of the entire organization and relying only on technology and not investing a proper amount of care and ownership in our Information Security Management efforts, any financial investment would end up being a waste.

We should manage uncertainty by using probability to lower probability

CHAPTER SUMMARY

Although the business mindset directs us toward believing that we can only determine the importance of processes or assets by quantifying them it is actually the elements of a business that are not quantifiable that account for the largest portion of risk. Apart from the lack of understanding and attention, the biggest challenge of investing in information security comes from the inability to accurately decide how much we are going to invest in something that we cannot accurately measure. This does not however mean that we should forget about counting the costs and the benefits or think that investments do not create benefits. It just means that we should, instead of monetizing the benefits, accept them as they are—very important, overwhelming, unquantifiable, but still proportional to the investment.

SELF-ASSESSMENT/DISCUSSION QUESTIONS

1. If you were to rate the importance of Confidentiality, Integrity, and Availability for your organization, what percentage of your entire Information Security would be given to each of the principles?
2. Does your organization inform its clients about data breaches that might affect them?
3. Do you have a disaster recovery site with duplicated, independently hosted crucial ICT systems that is located away from the original business site?
4. Would you rate your organization as agile according to the time period between a new threat has emerged, and until it was identified and addressed with actual measures?

5. How much effort and resources do you invest in mitigating internal risks, whether they are malicious or not?
6. Does your model of governance take into account the obligation to comply with local regulations?
7. Do you collect and analyze metrics that are being shared within your industry?
8. How frequently do you perform a thorough BIA?
9. Do you believe that the communication between all those that are concerned with security, especially the security function and decision makers, is effective and productive in your organization?
10. Do you invest the biggest part of thought and funds in finding and maintain skilled labor or identifying and purchasing technology?

References

[1] Identity Theft Report Center, ITRC Data Breach Reports—2015 Year-End Totals <http://www.idtheftcenter.org/ITRC-Surveys-Studies/2015databreaches.html>, 2016.

[2] IBM/ Ponemon, Cost of Data Breach Study <http://www-03.ibm.com/security/data-breach/>, 2016.

[3] Price Waterhouse Coopers, The Global State of Information Security Survey <http://www.pwccn.com/webmedia/doc/635948562625784617_rcs_info_security_2016.pdf>, 2016.

[4] Microsoft Advanced Threat Analytics <https://www.microsoft.com/en-us/cloud-platform/advanced-threat-analytics>.

[5] ISACA, Global Cybersecurity Status Report <http://www.isaca.org/pages/cybersecurity-global-status-report.aspx>, 2015.

[6] Trustwave, Global Security Report <https://www2.trustwave.com/rs/815-RFM-693/images/2015_TrustwaveGlobalSecurityReport.pdf>, 2015.

Organize

CHAPTER 7

Influencing Performance: Running an Efficient Security Organization

UNDERSTANDING EFFICIENCY

In this chapter we talk about making security more efficient. However, there is a big difference in how business leaders and those that are tasked to produce actual results understand efficiency. Simply, for business leaders, efficiency is often just another word for cheap. On the other hand, for security professionals, efficiency implies good performance regardless of cost. Naturally, and actually correctly, business leaders focus on costs while security professionals focus on performance. Basically, in order to make an educated decision, we are required to assess numerous layers of an issue, look at it from different sides, and challenge different, even opposing objectives against it. The actual problem is that security and business do not assess issues together but separately. Security will invent and propose strategies without thinking about their cost while the business leadership will immediately dismiss them as too expensive without analyzing the benefits. Actually, business will often classify security spending as too high based on a simply hunch and not as the result of a thorough Cost and Benefit analysis. The other usual model is that security will simply be granted a certain budget without being given a chance to influence it, but will eventually be required to produce tangible results with what it has. Efficiency is actually only achieved through a close collaboration between skill and cash and their joint decision that is the result of equal opportunities to present and defend and in the actual time spent together in analyzing, challenging, and deciding. Naturally, one of the important preconditions for security to be able to really influence top decisions is the place in the hierarchy of the organization that allows it to productively collaborate, present, defend, and show results, which is often not the case. In this chapter, I want to unite the two understandings of the term efficiency into one concept and analyze the elements that are necessary in order to have a successful security organization in an enterprise, both in terms of cost efficiency and performance.

From Corporate Security to Commercial Force. DOI: http://dx.doi.org/10.1016/B978-0-12-805149-8.00007-8

For business leaders, efficiency is often just another word for cheap while for security professionals, efficiency implies good performance regardless of cost.

THE ROLE OF BUSINESS LEADERSHIP

Security of an organization is the mirror image of the involvement of its leadership. Let us face it, it is the business leadership that is responsible for the security of a company while security managers only try to do their best to achieve maximum performance in, usually unfavorable circumstances that they did not create. We often say that security is as good as its weakest link. However, the weakest part of the security system of an organization is not the unmotivated and unskilled security guard at the entrance to the facility but a business leader that spends a bit of money on security so that he would not have to spend his valuable time thinking about it. We can even go as far as comparing investments in security with charity. In many cases, giving money to a charity cause is far from being sufficient and basically not really about making a change but more about washing own hands, satisfying conscience, and achieving peace of mind.

> Security of an organization is the mirror image of the involvement of its leadership.

MOTIVE, OPPORTUNITY, AND MEANS

Earlier in the book, we have mentioned Motive, Opportunity, and Means as the three elements that are required for a crime to occur. These elements are actually essential in order to perform basically any intentional activity, whether malicious or not. For me, Motivation, Opportunity, and Means are the three basic conditions that are necessary for the good functioning of any process, security included. I actually often like to jointly refer to these three elements as the Mom Triad because the same principles conveniently also play a very important role in successful parenting.

> Motivation, Opportunity and Means are the three basic conditions that are necessary for of any process.

Motivation

By Motivation, I do not mean incentives. Motivation to perform an activity comes from the perceived potential of that activity to actually make a difference. Consequently, it is also built through results, but also through acknowledgment and recognition of achievement. We know that employees need to be motivated through the recognition of their successes but when it comes to security, we usually acknowledge a winning strategy with "he was just doing his job." It is a stigma that the brains of security professional are wired differently than those of other employees and that they basically do not need an occasional pat on the back. Second, motivation comes from the ability to actually use knowledge and skills to solve challenging problems instead of simply servicing the needs of superiors that sometimes have nothing to do with actual security. Moreover, the key difference between a good security professional and a bad one is not necessarily technical knowledge but creativity to find simple solutions for complex problems. Business Leaders rarely see security as a creative function but more as utility service that simply follows business strategies and fills blanks by taking practical measures from a shelf and just applying them. Consequently, the tasks given to the security function often lack creativity and challenge, apart from the challenge to save costs and the need to exercise creativity in producing results without being given the tools.

> Just like all other employees, the motivation of security professionals is also built through acknowledgment and recognition of achievements.

Opportunity

The opportunity to perform starts with the understanding of business leaders of the importance of security for the business. This understanding is naturally the key factor when it comes to positioning security in the hierarchy of the organization, both vertically and horizontally. The vertically high position of security will give it the opportunity to directly communicate, present, and defend strategies to decision makers. Also, instead of being assigned to one part of the business, a security function that is positioned high will have a better overview of the entire business and all its processes. As such, it will be able to identify and solve actual problems and attend to issues that really require attention instead of concentrating on a small part of the organization that it organizationally belongs to. Actually, security is rarely positioned based on need but mostly based on convenience. In practice, that frequently results in performing unrelated tasks in its sector and neglecting real security issues in the rest of the company.

By vertical positioning, I mean independence and the ability to exercise objectivity. The security function will only be able to address vulnerabilities if it is as an effective control function that is not blocked by internal conflicts of interest. In many, even most cases, the security department and other departments that it controls report to the same function. For instance, Chief Information Security Officers (CISOs) typically report to the Head of the ICT Sector (Chief Information Officer, CIO). Naturally, the task of the CISO is to assess the effectiveness of ICT, report flaws, suggest improvements, and implement them following a decision and accompanying budgets. However, as the CISO is basically tasked to challenge the achievements of the function that he actually reports to, his assessments are not likely to pass beyond his superior. This consequently means that there is significantly less chance that budgets will be approved and that any actual improvements will be made.

Means

Means require a budget but are also far more reaching than a simple investment. Means actually involve all the tools that a security function uses to perform its activities. Naturally, it includes equipment but also knowledge, currentness, skilled people, access to information, and the actual ability to control and communicate.

> Means include equipment but also knowledge, currentness, skilled people, access to information and the actual ability to control, communicate and influence.

Information is the primary tool of Security. Efficient security needs to have the ability to collect and match timely and accurate information about company's decisions, and deep understanding of its strategies, processes, and directions with information about vulnerabilities and probable threats. The precondition is certainly that security is organizationally placed in a way that it will be able to receive firsthand critical information from decision makers. Second, it requires the ability to be up-to-date through professional networking, by participating in forums, and through professional seminars and courses. Logically, all these elements require both understanding and funds.

The link between budget and tools, as well as the link between tools and the ability of security to see, hear, and control, is quite clear. However, what is not often understood is how the lack of financial investment influences authority. Lack of investment in security is not only a serious obstacle for the practical operations of security but also a clear sign for company's employees that security is not important. I often think about the case of the security department in a large international bank in Bulgaria several years ago whose members had to use public transport when responding to emergencies in bank's branches around the country.

Of course, the tendency of some business to invest in technology and neglect other essentials of a security system carries the risk of neglecting skill, logic, and flexibility of security which are its most important elements and becoming the slave of tools instead of being their master.

> Lack of investment in security will be a clear sign for company's employees that security is not important.

BUDGET

Budget is important. It buys tools, attracts and keeps talent, and makes a statement. The usual problem related to security budgets, apart from amounts, is how they are approved and allocated. The people that approve security budgets are often even not the people that practically experience risks and enjoy security benefits. It is quite common that a local security department receives a budget according to a decision from a distance, that is sometimes made by people that never set foot in the facility, or even country, and know nothing about local circumstances. On top of that, the actual budget proposal forms are usually reduced to few simple columns that only allow naming a service or measure and its cost but rarely give the option to explain and justify proposed investments. Certainly, it is also very unlikely that a decision maker will have the time and the drive to read and assess lengthy budget proposals and actually make educated decisions based on real needs.

> The usual problem related to security budgets, apart from amounts, is how they are approved and allocated.

Probably the biggest problem is how budgets are allocated. There are only rare organizations where there is a separate security budget so that security can actually receive the resources that it needs without risking that the money will be used for other purposes. In practice, the budget that is proposed by the security function will be reduced by the function that it reports to so that it would match its larger budget proposal. Naturally, the next function that is higher in the hierarchy will do the same. When a budget is finally approved after several rounds of shortening, security will be granted just a fraction of what it originally asked for. Moreover, it will usually receive only a part of what was approved, as much of it will typically be used by the higher function for sudden unrelated quick-win projects with higher exposure.

Cataloging Services and Cost

It would not be fair not to mention also the frequent flaws in proposing budgets that are the responsibility of the security function. Knowing what are the services that we use and what are the funds that should support them seems like an easy mission. However, depending on the complexity of the organization, that mission might require quite a bit of thought. Security is certainly a complex function that operates beyond the walls of the security office and extends horizontally and vertically through the organization. The security function must always have an updated catalog of assets, services, and costs (including regulatory costs) in order to be able to propose budgets and basically manage the security of a company. On top of that, an important aspect for creating a budget is the list of vulnerabilities that should be addressed. The measures to address vulnerabilities should be categorized in terms of importance (must have, should have, and nice to have), cost (high, medium, and low), type of cost (fixed, variable, and investment), time required to implement measures (one year, two years, etc.), and time required for the return of investment. A successful security manager will always be able to name all the assets and processes that he/she is responsible for, show, and explain all the costs of security, be able to accurately present the status of current projects and elaborate future ones, explain vulnerabilities, and know the status of the security budget.

> Knowing what are the services that we use and what are the funds that should support them might require quite a bit of thought.

SECURITY ORGANIZATION

Creating an effective security program in your organization starts with staffing a team of innovative and smart people to support the security mission. The structure and size of a security team and the profiles of its members depend on many factors such as the budget, the industry, the nature of the business (product, service, or mixed orientation), the type of business, and the business's product, core processes, vulnerabilities, and location and whether the business is a single or multisite operation. Certainly, it is always more important to have a coherent team that is working toward a common goal than a big group of excellent individuals who are working independently.

> It is always better to have a small team with a common goal than a big group of excellent independent individuals.

A typical division of professional security pillars in a security organization is based on specific skills and experience required for a certain field of security. Naturally, what parts of the organization will be reserved for a certain pillar depend on the importance of that segment in the particular company. Basically, there is a big difference between expertise, job descriptions, importance, and attention given to an ICT security professional in a small hotel and in a large bank, including the number of professionals required to manage the process successfully.

When we create a security setup, we base it on several elements: the industry, the nature of the business (product, service, or mixed orientation), the type of business, product, core processes, vulnerabilities, and location and whether the business is a single or multisite operation. The starting point is certainly the industry, main assets, product, and risks associated with it.

For instance, bank's main assets are information systems and networks; the main product is electronic money while the most common risks are high-tech crimes, computer-crimes, frauds that are mostly committed electronically, and business discontinuity. Naturally, the main accent when creating a team will be put on information security, fraud and business continuity management, and disaster recovery. In case of a small local bank, we might decide to have one person in charge of managing all three main types of risk by closely cooperating with other departments. For example, the ICT department will assist the Chief Information Security Officer (CISO) by executing the technical part of information security and the information dimension of business continuity while Internal Audit will help with fraud controls and investigations. Together with that, the physical security manager will be in charge of the physical security of the bank, manned guarding, physical security technology, cash in transit, the physical aspect of business continuity, and the safety of bank's executives.

In a large international bank, we will usually have a Security Vice President function that will be in charge of both information and physical security on the global level and assisted by the CISO and the Chief Security Officer (CSO). A CISO will typically manage a team of experts, such as information security engineer, Information security governance, business continuity and disaster recovery manager, and fraud prevention and investigation specialist. On the side of physical security, the team reporting to the CSO will, depending on the complexity and the risks, consist of Regional Security Managers (EMEA, APAC, NA, and LATAM), and a position in charge of global executive protection and duty of care. On the affiliate level, again depending on the size and complexity, a local security team will typically be supervised by a national security director (National CSO) and consist of a CISO, physical security specialist, business continuity and disaster recovery manager, and a fraud prevention expert.

In product-oriented enterprises, where the main risks are associated with the physical product instead of information security and fraud, we will usually not have a separate function that deals exclusively with fraud prevention, while information security related functions might be merged. On the other hand, we might decide to have separate functions that manage specific risks that are associated with different stages of the product lifecycle, such as the Supply Chain Security Manager and Retail Loss Prevention Manager. Naturally, the best way to create a new security function would always be to hire a professional security consultant that would be able to assess all the processes, assets, and needs and suggest the adequate setup.

However, building a security team is a far more complex task than simply gathering security professionals who specialize in various fields of security.

An engine (a team) is much more than many independent parts (members), regardless of their quality. When building a team, we usually concentrate on several features that are crucial for team dynamics [1]:

- Performance (right position at a right time doing right things in the right way)—It basically means that you have the person with relevant skills for the position, at the right moment in his career, who is appropriately instructed concerning his tasks and has the ability to execute them.
- Best for the team—You want a person who will fit in the team like a piece of a puzzle but at the same time motivate the team. It is not unusual or wrong to involve the other team members in assessing a potential newcomer to the team.
- A communicator—Good communication is essential for the team and the management and for dealing with issues at an early stage. You do not have a team unless the members are effectively communicating
- Character—You are employing not only a professional but also a person with whom you and other team members are going to interact.

EMPLOYMENT CRITERIA

No company is rich enough to hire cheap security. Actually, the biggest portion of the security budget should be reserved for the people and not for technology as it is often the case. When it comes to hiring, in the case of the chicken and egg causality dilemma there is actually no dilemma—the egg always comes before the chicken. Basically, it depends on the egg that we buy, what kind of chicken will grow out of it. However, making a right decision requires knowledge and skill. The first mistake that we make is how we generally conceptualize and run the hiring process for expert functions, especially security. The hiring criteria for the security function are usually determined by the business leadership of the company, the search is performed by a general placement contractor, and the process is finalized by Human Resources. Typically, the functions that run the hiring process know absolutely nothing about setting the requirements for the security function and how to really make an educated hiring decision. Probably the best and the simplest way to hire smart and suitable is to contract a placement agency that specializes in hiring security professionals and involve it in the entire process, from setting the criteria to choosing the right candidate.

Many times, the accent when hiring a security professional is put on education. Actually, formal education is often presented as the unit of measure. For instance—one degree equals 10 years of experience. However, in security, nothing can replace practical experience, not even education. Sometimes, the requirement is in not even a relevant degree but basically any formal degree. Still, a formal relevant degree should only be a valuable addition that rounds-up experience. Second, in my opinion, professional society issued certifications are often given more weight than they actually deserve in the overall calculus of a hiring decision. Instead of being regarded as an advantage they are usually viewed as the main criteria and the ultimate proof of knowledge, skill and abilities, and assurance of performance.

> Typically, the functions that run the hiring process for the security function don't know enough about it to make an educated hiring decision.

Certainly, apart from making sure that a candidate possesses relevant knowledge and experience, we want to hire people that are well connected to the industry and have access to best practices and do not only rely on their own creativity. Also, one of the most important tools of security is the ability to efficiently communicate. The language capabilities, understanding and appropriately responding to the unique combination of cultural variables, and fitting in the demographic structure of the company are vital for the overall success of the security function in any commercial organization. Simply, if security people are likely to privately socialize with others, they will work better together and produce better results. Finally, security needs to use business acumen when designing security strategies and has to be able to understand and speak the language of the business in order to communicate them and defend them.

POSITIONING SECURITY

We did come to the conclusion that one of the main conditions for the better functioning of security requires independence, ability to exercise objectivity and hierarchical opportunities to communicate with stakeholders, and influence their opinion, but also be influenced and directed by them so that security strategies will follow the direction of the business. Naturally, as security is a companywide service, it is logical that the CSO should report to the CEO instead to the Head of Operations, or in case of a CISO to the CIO. Actually, we will achieve the best results by regarding overall security as a concept and not only as functions and by uniting physical and information security under one roof that reports directly to the CEO or the Board of Directors. However, the benefits would not only be operational but also very financial. Although there are practically no studies that analyze the financial benefits of positioning physical security directly under the CEO, there are studies that do quantify the line of reporting of information security in companies. Still, we can confidently apply the findings also to physical security and basically to the entire converged security department. According to the "2014 Global State of

Information Security Survey" conducted by PriceWaterhouseCoopers on more than 9000 international respondents, organizations where the CISOs report to CIOs have 14% more downtime due to security incidents [2]. According to the same study, in such organizations, information security related financial losses are 46% higher than in organizations where the CISO reports to the CEO [2]. Actually, in some technologically advanced countries, for instance in Israel, laws require that CISOs report directly to the CEO.

> There is usually more security related downtime and more losses in organizations where security doesn't report directly to the CEO.

PEOPLE

While the role of security management of the company is to lead the security efforts of a company, it is the employees that are the actual security of the company. However, the involvement of people in the security system does not only depend on their will to contribute but on how they perceive the importance of security for themselves. The high paced business playground often forces employees to decide between getting their work done on time and following security procedures that might waste that time. The trade-off is quite clear—to do the right thing and risk losing the job, or get the job done and probably not suffer any consequences for security flaws. While security uses various methods to communicate, influence, and convince, the real influence comes from noticing that it is actually really important for the company and that it is part of the job. Signs and emails will be completely ineffective unless the leadership of the company supports and emphasizes security and actively participates in it, the investment in security is adequate and visible, and if secure behavior is rewarded and failures are punished just like flaws in performing regular work tasks. People notice double standards and know when something is important for them.

> The involvement of people in the security system depends on how they perceive the importance of security for themselves.

Gamification of Security Awareness

While the route to punishment is quite clear and its outcome is never fun, becoming a valuable part of the security system can actually be entertaining for employees, besides being worthwhile in terms of actual rewards. Since few years there is a new trend of building security awareness through game-like activity. While the trend started in information security, it is quickly spreading further to all aspects of security. The idea of Security Awareness Gamification relies on several principles. It should be fun, participation should be voluntary, it needs to have clear rules and goals, and success must be rewarded. The principle of security awareness games is actually quite similar to collecting frequent-flyer miles. Basically, employees receive and accumulate points by exercising secure behavior, reporting security flaws, or for instance participating in a security training. Naturally, different activities carry different points while failures take points away. Eventually, the employees that were able to collect the required number of points will receive a reward. Of course, the model (or amount) of the reward would depend on the ranking.

TECHNOLOGY

It would be irresponsible to label technology as not important. However, we are often so impressed by technology that we attempt to replace all aspects of security with technological solutions. Moreover, we often neglect other important particulars by over-relying on shiny blinking boxes. First of all, there is no technology that can replace skilled people, it can only actually improve their performance, and only if people and technology are carefully blended. Second, the simplest solutions are usually the most effective ones. For example, the greatest security invention and the element that probably deserves the most credit for preventing and stopping the biggest number security incidents is actually a simple locked door. We also tend to take technology for granted and rarely ask ourselves if really need it and is there something that we can use instead, or something that we can combine it with, that can make it both more effective and cheaper. For example, in order to prevent robberies, most banks have expensive interlocking systems at the entrance to their branches that are able to sustain an explosion. However, not only that a bombing attack is not at all probable during a bank robbery, branches in most cases do not even have procedures and practical abilities to notice criminal intent and prevent a potential perpetrator from entering nor will they attempt to stop a criminal after he has committed the robbery. Also, every bank robber knows that all interlocking doors have the possibility to be opened together for the case of evacuation and that every bank teller will gladly open both doors if threatened. However, as the idea behind interlocking doors is to simply deter a robber in the phases of planning by warning him that his entry and escape will be slow, any cheaper system that can delay entry, such as simple rotating doors, would be as effective. It is also in many cases possible to mix technology solutions and physical means in order to save costs and achieve even better results. One such example is combining CCTV cameras with mirrors which can drastically reduce the number of required expensive cameras. Basically, instead of saving costs by applying technological solutions we could actually save much more by questioning their efficiency and relevance before running to the store.

We often neglect other parts of security by over-relying on shiny blinking boxes.

COMMUNICATION

As the role of security is to lead the security efforts of a company according to the information that it receives and collects, and information that it passes, communication is the crucial feature of a corporate security organization. Security needs to have the opportunity to effectively communicate upwards with the leadership of the entity, vertically with other functions, and downwards with basically all the employees in the organization. We have already stressed the importance of the proper positioning of security in an organization for the communication with the upper management. Moreover, the position naturally also stimulates the influence of security thought the company. Basically, security has to be officially entitled and recognized by others as eligible. One of the most effective ways in which the security function interacts with other vertical functions is not only through common projects but also through scheduled recurring face-to-face meetings that do not have a strict agenda and where both functions can explore new ideas instead of only solving existing issues. Of course, for other functions to allocate time and cooperate with security beyond simply addressing immediate needs, they have to understand that security is important and that they will benefit from closer interaction.

To be able to effectively communicate, security has to be officially entitled and recognized by others as eligible.

CHAPTER SUMMARY

There are no two organizations that are the same. Naturally, it would be irresponsible to suggest one universal model that would improve the efficiency of security in all the different circumstances. However, there are rules that are applicable in most, if not all organizations. Security is a company-wide process that has to be provided with the opportunity to influence the corporate leadership and be influenced by it which can only be done by positioning security close to the decision maker. Moreover, while it is absolutely crucial that security interacts and works together with other functions, it should remain independent from these functions and have an equal voice in the discussion without being blocked by conflicts of interests and conflicts of budget. Finally, security can only work when it is part of the strategic direction of the company, when it is supported, emphasized, and followed by its leadership, and when all the employees understand that doing their part in the security efforts of a company is practically and personally important for them and do not regard it as a purely philosophical concept.

SELF-ASSESSMENT/DISCUSSION QUESTIONS

1. Does your organization invest thoughts, efforts, and funds in increasing the motivation of your security function, providing opportunities that it requires, and acquiring means that are necessary for its performance?
2. In terms of budget and lines of reporting, is the security function in your organization independent and able to exercise objectivity?
3. Does the security function in your company receive direct and timely updates on strategic decisions, new processes, and projects?
4. Do the decision makers in your company perceive security as competent enough to influence business decisions?
5. Do functions in your organization see security as their equal partner?
6. Can employees in your organization establish a clear link between company's security and their personal goals?
7. When hiring security professionals, does your company involve specialized security placement agencies in the employment process?
8. Does the security function in your organization frequently schedule brainstorming meetings with all other vertical functions?

References

[1] M. Cabric, Corporate Security Management. Challenges, Risks, and Strategies, Butterworth-Heinemann, Oxford, 2015, pp. 38–39.

[2] Price Waterhouse Coopers, The Global State of Information Security Survey <http://www.pwc.com/gx/en/consulting-services/information-security-survey/pwc-gsiss-2014-key-findings-report.pdf>, 2014.

CHAPTER 8

Costs Saving and Cost Avoidance:
Security as the Usual Suspect

MISCONCEPTIONS ABOUT SAVING ON SECURITY

In many cases, businesses are not even completely aware of the core benefits of their security, and are often sacrificing resilience for profit. They will often choose to save costs instead of protecting profit and assets. Basically, while the financial benefits of saving on security are felt immediately and are easily quantifiable, in order to experience the downside of the lack of security, we have to wait for an incident to happen, sometimes for a long time. Moreover, we usually cannot predict its consequences. Unfortunately, the high paced business playground and the need to make business decisions based on tangible and easily quantifiable educated guesses point to the direction of accepting the risks and going with the profit. As such, it is, in case of many businesses, unrealistic to expect that they would allocate time and invest resources to thoroughly analyze the indirect benefits of their security unless these benefits are quantifiable, undoubtedly commercial, and would substantially increase profits.

> Quantifiable guesses point to the direction of accepting security risks.

Why is security the first choice when it comes to saving costs? Probably the biggest mistake that we make when conceptualizing security is to think about it as something that we buy instead of something that we create or something that is nice to have instead of something that we need. Therefore, when thinking about lowering security related expenses, we naturally save on it instead of optimizing it. We often underestimate the importance of security for the business. Consequently, one of the biggest fallacies when it comes to saving on security is believing that we are able to change the nature of security expenses from Fixed Expenses to Variable Costs and in that way lower production expenses without affecting the actual product. Moreover, instead of using security as a tool that could positively influence the business and reflect on the bottom line, we usually use security cost saving as magic remedy that will cover bad business results.

> The biggest mistake that we make when conceptualizing security is to think about it as something that we buy instead of something that we create.

From Corporate Security to Commercial Force. DOI: http://dx.doi.org/10.1016/B978-0-12-805149-8.00008-X

Certainly, if our intention is to save simply for the sake of achieving greater profit, we should definitively reconsider. The paradox is that with the increase of profit, our security needs will also proportionally increase. Although we often believe that saving on security is entirely a business decision, it should actually be a decision that is based on a joint assessment performed by business and the security function together, as the damaged effectiveness of security and organizational resilience might actually end up costing more than the original setup before saving. Finally, as security is a service that is put upfront, and often the first point of contact between our business and our customers, saving on security will not go unnoticed. Actually, for our clients and partners, cheaper security could be a sign that the business is in trouble.

> For our clients and partners, cheaper security could be a sign that the business is in trouble.

UNDERSTANDING BUSINESS EXPENSES

Bookkeeping and accounting systems track activities by assigning each recurring expense to a particular account. The accounts are all given a number of defining attributes and among those is a designation of fixed expense or variable expense. This is important because most business planning activities require that expenses be easily segregated into these two categories. For business, it is crucial to track and understand expenses, and especially their nature, origin and influence, in order to be able to efficiently plan, forecast, invest, and save.

Expenses in a corporation can be divided into two main categories:

- Recurring Expenses (Operating Expenses / OPEX)
- Nonrecurring Expenses (Capital Expenditure / CAPEX)

Recurring Expenses

Recurring Expenses are ongoing expenses required for operating a company. Typically, they include things such as raw materials and logistics, salaries, rent and bills, research and development costs, travel and related expenses, computer support services, etc.

The two main types of recurring expenses are:

- Fixed Expenses
- Variable Expenses

Fixed Expenses are the ones that are included in the cost of the production and shape the price of the product but do not change with the volume of production and are more or less fixed. Basically, regardless of the production volume, the cost of the security service will stay the same. In general, employees and office equipment also fall under Fixed Manufacturing Costs.

Variable Expenses (or Costs) are also included in the price of the product but change with the changes in the production volume. For example, Variable Costs can be associated with the shipment packaging of the product. If the company produces less, it will also require less packaging. Basically, Variable Costs will always be included in the cost of a product in the same, or similar percentage. Variable Costs are also associated with, for example, part-time outsourced staff that is required to complete a certain project. In general, the smaller the volume, the less external staff will be required to produce it.

Nonrecurring Expenses

Nonrecurring expenses (Capital Expenses/Capex) are expenses where the benefit continues over a long period, rather than being exhausted in a short period. Such expenditure is of a nonrecurring nature and results in acquisition of permanent assets. Capital Expenses are typically investments in tangible assets that add value to the business and are usually associated with technology and physical parameters of the premises. With Capital Expenses, a company will basically raise its value, improve processes, and, should the business be sold, the investments will be returned.

SECURITY EXPENSES

Security as Fixed Expense

Unfortunately, security falls under the most unpopular accounting category. The cost of security is fixed and does not change with the volume, and presumably does not actually add value to the product. According to the business, while employees are in general a Fixed Expense, the ones that are engaged in the core business or directly supporting it, are certainly part of the product and counting them in the cost of the product makes sense. Professional Human Capital is also the asset that will add value to the price of the company should it be sold. However, the presumption is that while other employees, services, and costs actually shape the product, security only protects it and does not contribute to its actual production not does it directly add value to it. Basically, for the business management, not investing in security or even making it redundant is the preferred way of cutting production costs without affecting the actual production, the product, and the value of the business. Security is often perceived as unnecessary cost that could be used as additional financial space in case there is a need to save costs or invest in other services that are more relevant for the core business.

While similarly, the cost of Environment, Health, and Safety (EHS or HSE) is also included in operational costs but still does not influence the product, unlike security EHS is protected by laws and regulations and cannot be saved on.

> The cost of security is fixed and doesn't change with the volume, and presumably does not actually add value to the product.

Transferring Security Related Costs from Fixed to Capital Expenses

For many enterprises, investing in security technology seems to be the perfect solution; as for the initial investment is a Capital Expense and not a Fixed Expense. While equipment maintenance will be a reoccurring expense, the cost of maintenance would still be much lower than people related expenses.

Unfortunately, when thinking where to cut the costs, business stakeholder will not spend valuable time analyzing security in order to come up with the conclusion that technology and people are together with procedures, physical elements, communication, information, and management essential founding elements of a security system. Basically, security companies call the particular elements of security that they are selling "Solutions" and are actually managing to convince their clients that what they are offering are complete security solutions (whether they are only selling technology or manned guarding service). Naturally, if a business is forced to cut the costs and still have security in one form or another, it will often opt for the cheapest solution and chose technology over people believing that in that way it would lower the expenses and remove them from fixed expenses while the level of security will stay the same or that its efficiency will even increase.

Transferring Security Related Costs from Fixed to Variable Expenses

Changing the nature of the entire security cost from a fixed expense to a variable cost, although possible in theory, would be quite challenging in practice as it would require an outsourced security organization that would, based on the input from business, practically in real-time reduce or increase the number of outsourced employees according to changes in the production volume. First of all, as security setup does not depend solely on production volumes, it would not make much sense to increase or reduce the number of security personnel based on volume changes. Second, a security company would not be capable of instantly increasing their workforce as that would mean pulling employees from another site where they might be required, or employing and training additional employees that might become redundant after a short time. Finally, this fluctuation will undoubtedly negatively impact the performance of security and will certainly overshadow any potential, and probably minimal cost saving. This arrangement is, however, possible and even preferred in case of predicted longer lasting change of circumstances. For instance, a predicted drop in productivity or its growth which is expected to last for a longer period of time will justify the proportionally lower or higher spending on security. Also, a seaside resort will naturally recurrently increase its security during summer months and decrease it during winter.

> As security setup doesn't depend solely on production volumes, it wouldn't make much sense to increase or reduce the number of security personnel based on volume changes.

COMMERCIAL MINDSET VERSUS PROTECTION STRATEGIES

Position of Security Based on the Type of Expenses

The accounting method is also mostly responsible for the position of security in a corporation. If we take the examples of industrial corporations, security is usually placed in the Operations sector that is in charge of the production and responsible for expenses that are included in the cost of the product. However, the security department is responsible for the security of the entire company and not only for the assets and processes that fall under Operations. Even more so, it is not rare that because of the nature of a company and the type of risk that are associated with it, the security department should focus on riskier processes that are not the responsibility of Operations but the responsibility of, for example, Sales and Distribution, such as the Supply Chain and Retail. This actually leads to the paradox that Operations director has to justify high security costs for which he sees no value in his/her sector while the Sales Director has no security associated costs and still enjoys all the benefits. However, in reality, security functions will mostly focus on the processes in their sector, simply as their efforts will be more visible to their superiors and as their achievements will directly influence their performance appraisals. There is certainly much more of a performance and much less of a conflict in organizations where security reports directly to the CEO or is organizationally placed based on need and not based on accounting convenience. In that way, security will be more practical, it will be better in supporting the business while its benefits will be more visible which would justify spending.

> Security functions mostly focus on the processes in their sector, simply as their efforts are more visible to their superiors.

Strategic Planning in the Quick-Win Commercial Culture

Businesses are often very slow when it comes to making changes that are related to security, unless these changes have the potential to quickly save costs. Moreover, even security initiatives that would actually result in more significant savings and at the same time drastically improve processes, but have a longer return of investment, are usually not likely to be approved. Basically, the mobility of executive functions in corporations does not leave much space for long-term strategic planning. Top executives are mostly looking at quick wins and investments with a fast return of investments for processes that do not directly influence the product while they are naturally more tolerant when it comes to improving production efficiency and sales. Basically, every top executive prefers to invest into something that will give quick results during his/her mandate. Otherwise, he will report spending while his successor will report savings and benefits.

> Security initiatives that have a longer return of investment, are usually not likely to be approved.

However, the essence of security has nothing to do with the accounting method or its expense influenced position in the company but actually with its performance and cost efficiency in protecting tangible and intangible assets of the company and adding value to the processes and the product. It is clear that counting expenses and how much the cost of security adds to the cost of production is much easier than counting the benefits of security versus investment or even quantifying the role of security in preventing losses. Basically, because of its indirect influence on the entire business, quantifying security and quantifying losses are some of the most challenging security related tasks for a company.

COST SAVING AND COST AVOIDANCE

There are countless available economic studies that thoroughly explain the difference between Cost Saving and Cost Avoidance. However, instead of going deep into economics, I will practically explain the difference between the two on the actual example of Corporate Security. Certainly, both cost saving and cost avoidance aim at lowering operational costs. However, on one hand, Cost Saving simply reduces spending without tackling the cause of expenses. For instance, if company's sales did not produce expected results, the company could decrease the number of security guards in order to save costs. A company will usually not be able to save costs without impacting the performance of the function that it is saving on. On the other hand, Cost Avoidance typically requires an investment that would improve the process in a way that it would become more cost effective and still preserve or even improve the level of performance. For example, a bank could save on security associated costs by outsourcing security guards in its branches and installing cheap technology. Naturally, the more it would save on security, the lower the quality of security that it will get in return, whether as a result of bad performance or of the smaller number of people and/or equipment that are performing it. On the other hand, the bank could decide to avoid costs by replacing the guards with more expensive technological and physical elements that would require an initial investment but would end up being more effective end eventually much cheaper.

> Cost Avoidance typically requires an investment that would improve the process in a way that it would become more cost effective.

Avoiding Costs by Investing in Technology

Although I am not at all an advocate of replacing people with technology, in the particular case of a bank, it actually holds water. As I have mentioned in previous chapters, the presence of security guards in a bank branch functions purely as a presentation and practically has no real security significance. Certainly, if it is mostly about presentation, it is undoubtedly better to have no presentation than having a bad one. So, although we like to think that a criminal would be deterred by the presence of security, the truth is that criminals are as much aware as we are that the particular type of security personnel in bank branches usually has neither the ability to spot and prevent a crime nor the capability or mandate to react during an ongoing incident. Basically, robbers will not be concerned with who is going to be present during a robbery, but who will actually do something about it. On the other hand, revolving doors are perfect in assisting the security of a service oriented facility and discourage potential criminals without actually deterring clients. Basically, the inability to quickly enter and exit the facility would be a major downside for criminals and a factor that would most probably force them to choose another target. On the other hand, revolving doors are so widespread that they would not be a hustle for the regular clients of the bank. Apart from that, investing in modern IP CCTV technology that is supervised by well-trained operations center personnel would address numerous other issues ranging from regular security monitoring, preventing and detecting employee dishonesty, providing credible evidence footage following an incident and even performing administrative tasks, such as counting clients, and providing customer analytics. The system would certainly also require training clerks in security in fraud awareness, reaction during an incident and recovery. The bank could also, based on the thorough risk assessment of branches, decide to keep professional security personnel in certain branches. Moreover, because of the small much number of security personnel that it would require, it would be able to handpick the security officers and actually concentrate on their performance. So, as much as this system would require an initial investment, it would end up being much cheaper and much more efficient than any traditional manned guarding setup would have been.

> In cases when security is mostly about presentation, it is undoubtedly better to have no presentation than to have a bad one.

Avoiding Costs by Performing Risk Assessments

If we take the example of Models of Corporate Governance, the Centralized Model is losing the battle to the Federal Model. Basically, according to the Federal Model of Corporate Governance, all the separate parts of the business are able to match their circumstances with general standards and create applicable procedures and rules instead of trying to apply detailed imposed rules that might not be applicable or practical. The same principle goes for security. Instead of trying to find a perfect formula for a security setup that would be applicable everywhere, every place deserves special attention. Actually, apart from being the most convenient and the least time consuming, the method of arranging any process according to a strict rule rather than according to specific circumstances will end up being costlier and less efficient. We can take a chain of retail stores in one city as an example. Certainly, we will take into account the parameters such as the size, type of products that are being sold in stores, location, and traffic. One of the important parameters is also vulnerability. While the type of risks that is associated with all the stores is pretty much the same, the circumstances and vulnerabilities are quite different. For instance, when we assess the probability of an incident, we do not only look at the theoretical dimension of security risk, but more importantly the practical possibility that these risks can actually turn into incidents. So, while the overall risk could be robbery, numerous parameters will determine which stores would actually be attractive for the robbers in terms of access, action, and efficient escape. Applying one rule to different circumstances will most probably result in some units lacking performance, some exceeding the needs and being more expensive than necessary, while only a limited number of units will have the optimal performance and consequently the optimal ratio between cost and actual need. While a thorough professional assessment and basing a security setup upon it would be an investment, it would certainly have a short ROI and would result in both significant savings and better performance.

> Applying one rule to different circumstances will most probably result in some units lacking performance and some exceeding necessary costs.

Avoiding Costs by Investing in People

Although I am a security professional, or maybe because I am one, if I would have to choose between having a cheap security department or instead, investing that amount in security awareness trainings for nonsecurity employees, I would in most cases choose the later. This is especially the case with service oriented business such as retail, hospitality, and financial services. Basically, it is obvious that investing in security motivation, awareness, and emergency communication of hotel employees would be much more efficient than investing the same amount in a security setup, whether it consists of security officers, technology, or the combination of both.

Case Study: Budgeting Exercises

During my courses on Security Economics to hotel managers, I usually perform a budgeting exercise. During the initial brainstorming prior to the exercise, the participants voice their opinions on investing in security and overwhelmingly speak in favor of investing in security technology and security officers that are operating it. When the actual exercise starts, participants are asked to create a sustainable security setup for a hotel based on the budget that they receive. I usually divide the participants into three groups where all the participants receive the same detailed description of the hotel and a list of all possible security measures that they could implement but each of the groups receives a different budget that they are allowed to spend on it. Naturally, one group receives a very small budget, one receives optimal budget, while the third one is awarded a very high budget. Each of the security measures that they could use is realistically priced and described in terms of its actual possibilities and limits, and what additional spending might be required in order to use it (e.g., when installing video surveillance, it requires people that will operate it). It is very interesting that, as opposed to the initial points of view on security measures, all three groups always end up "investing" the biggest part of the budget in regular nonsecurity employees, especially in training, drills, and exercises, improved routine and emergency communication, security awareness rewards for staff, etc. They also opt for Crime Prevention Through Environmental Design (CPTED) techniques such as arranging the physical design in a way that it would deter criminals and enable better visibility and still be visually appealing to guests. As for the core security measures, they would mostly choose a small but handpicked professional manned guarding service instead of a larger but cheaper security organization. All three groups would also use (mostly free) services that would enable them to be up-to-date with risks, such as joining security forums, maintaining close contacts with law enforcement, and being able to be always timely informed on happenings that could influence their security.

Surprisingly, all three groups would usually allocate the least portion of the budget on purchasing security technology.

THE IMPACT OF CORPORATE COST SAVING ON THE MODUS OPERANDI OF TERRORISM

The Changing Modus Operandi of Terrorism

In recent years, Jihadist terrorism has transformed from highly centralized organizations that carefully plan and execute actions from "top to bottom" to a looser concept that encourages, and mostly relies on "home-grown" terrorists and lone wolfs. There are several reasons for that. First of all, the surprise effect is gone, and it is now much harder for terrorist organizations to execute another 9/11; tighter surveillance makes it more difficult for terrorists to communicate and effectively coordinate actions; homeland security organizations are becoming more serious and more determined to raise the level of security on a national level and protect critical infrastructure. Basically, it is now more difficult to perform attacks against government institutions (they can still use cyber terrorism against those), than it was 10 years ago. So, target hardening is actually giving results. Unfortunately, the results did not really tackle the number of terrorist attacks or the number of casualties but have only changed the way in which terrorist organizations work. Every security professional knows that the aim of target hardening is not to completely root out global terrorism or crime as it would be an impossible mission, but to simply send it elsewhere. So where did it go? Actually not that far at all. It only moved next door from harder national targets to much softer, but equally rewarding business targets. So, not only that it is much easier to execute an attack in a hotel or Shopping Mall than against an embassy, it is also more rewarding in terms of the probable number of civilian victims and media coverage.

Security, Profit, and Vulnerability

The goal and the core business of homeland security organizations is security and they are determined to mitigate security risks. For companies, the goal is profit while security (if they even have any) is merely a support function that should ensure it. For example, supermarkets do not care what you bring inside but only what you take out. And of course, security will make sense as long as the financial benefit of having it is higher than its cost. Companies are naturally determined to save costs and security is certainly on the top of the cost saving list. Unfortunately, it is exactly those marginalized security organizations that companies are saving on that are now at the forefront of the war against terrorism. Apart from simply saving costs on security and hoping that nothing will happen, one of the reasons for this negligence is also the cliché opinion that we have about terrorism and the conviction that it will only affect certain industries and only in certain areas. Actually, whether we are security professionals or laymen, we are addicted to simplifying terms and generalizing. Nowadays, bombing and shooting attacks are a fashion and we basically see terrorism as massive armed attacks against civilians that are motivated by ideology. However, for example, lethal poisoning of food in a big supermarket would also be terrorism, and not only that is it possible but very probable. Actually, it has been done in the past. Let us also not forget food and FMCG production, pharmaceuticals, or basically any production, sales or service that could be altered or used to facilitate terrorism or crime, or inflict damages directly.

> Marginalized security organizations are now at the forefront of the war against terrorism.

THE ROLE OF SECURITY IN LOWERING OPERATING COSTS

It is no brainer that if our security functions the way it should, it will lower the costly losses that we might have as a result of internal or external incidents. However, we would usually only classify as incidents the happenings that are separately able to cause great damage. In order to really see these benefits, we have to wait for an incident to actually happen so that we could quantify it. But what is the role of security in lowering operating costs? Amongst the assets that security is protecting are also operating assets such as tools, machines, materials used for production, inventory, office supplies, etc. Moreover, in many cases the majority of losses is not the result of big security incidents but of the consistent dripping of operating assets, whether as a result of irrational use, external crimes, employee dishonesty, or simply carelessness. Actually, it is exactly this prevention of leakage related to operating assets that is the main routine task of corporate security organizations. While we might indeed save costs on security and notice the direct financial benefits, we could be at the same time increasing our operating costs in a way that they will probably exceed the costs that we have had. Still, by dividing and diluting expenses through our bookkeeping and accounting systems, we are likely to, not only fail to establish a connection with saving on security, but actually completely miss it.

> Most losses are not the result of big security incidents but of the consistent dripping of operating assets.

CHAPTER SUMMARY

While saving costs is certainly one of the most widespread tools for increasing profitability it rarely remains a necessary one-time measure and often turns into a long-term strategy. Actually, cost saving is almost never a temporary action whose aim is to help the recovery of the business but a never ending process. Basically, if we have saved on a certain process, we will not revert to the previous setup once we recover. Moreover, should we again encounter problems in the future, we will most likely additionally save on the same processes that we have saved on in the past. While there are some corporate processes that have the capacity to withstand cost saving without being compromised in terms of the quality of performance, for security, lower cost almost always means lower performance. Certainly, because of its nature, security is amongst the first services that we think about when we plan to cut expenses. Inevitably, we will reach a stage where we pay for security more than we actually get from it as, although we will pay very little for it, we will receive nothing in return. Nevertheless, there are numerous strategies that can be implemented that will lower the costs and still not affect the performance. These strategies, however, require a close interaction between the business management and security management, presuming that the position of Chief Security Officer was not made redundant as part of previous cost saving initiatives.

SELF-ASSESSMENT/DISCUSSION QUESTIONS

1. Do you believe that you will save costs and improve the performance of your security by investing more in technology and less in people?
2. Are you trying to find the way to change the nature of security related costs in your company?
3. Do you mostly only cut security costs in your company or actually invest in optimization?
4. Do you optimize your security organization by performing thorough risk assessments?
5. What are the security measures that you would implement in your organization that almost do not involve spending?

CHAPTER 9

Security Outsourcing:
A Double-Edged Sword

INTRODUCTION

As much as in life, nothing should be taken for granted; in business, no critical decisions should be taken without thorough analyses. We live in the era of information and lack of time. As such, we often base important decisions on information, but do not invest enough time in thoroughly checking their credibility and relevance. We actually instinctively believe that by investing time in analyzing, we spend resources instead of simply saving. Although we are mostly aware that we must tailor our strategies to the specific requirements of our business, we frequently recklessly make choices based on the experience, and even rumors of others, even if there are absolutely no similarities between our and their industries, products, business models, goals, size, or location. If we regard security as being always completely detached from the business and without any real influence on it, it is logical that we would opt to outsource it without investing much thought in how outsourcing would reflect on its performance. The truth is that the more we save when we outsource, the more expensive security will turn out to be when compared to the actual support that the business receives from it. Finally, it will turn into a figure without performance before being completely dismissed. However, security is certainly one of the crucial processes that deserves special treatment. The more attention, time, and resources we invest in security, the more benefits we will receive from it, including actual security but also tangible benefits for core processes and the overall business, and consequently for the bottom line. There is a big difference between outsourcing gardening services, handing-over product packaging to an external company, or occasionally using a service provider for mailing holiday greeting cards and outsourcing a service that should ensure the security, safety, and integrity of our people, assets, products, processes, and information.

> We often make important decisions based on pieces of information without investing enough time in thoroughly checking their credibility and relevance.

From Corporate Security to Commercial Force. DOI: http://dx.doi.org/10.1016/B978-0-12-805149-8.00009-1

WHAT ARE PRIVATE SECURITY COMPANIES

Private security companies are enterprises that provide armed and/or unarmed security service and/or knowledge to clients. The largest part of the private security industry belongs to companies providing manned guarding services by deploying security guards (security officers) at their clients' facilities for the purpose of protecting people and assets. Manned guarding companies mostly deal with entry control, receptionist services, patrolling and stewarding, protection of cash in transit, operation of technical systems, fire protection, and prevention and detection of theft. Manned guarding companies often also provide bodyguard services, bouncer services, and guard dog services. Use of firearms by security guards in corporate security has, in many countries, greatly decreased in recent years as security systems are concentrating more on prevention than on reaction. Apart from the shift in the nature and perception of security, one reason is the lack of skill. The low cost of security services and the workforce fluctuation makes it hard for security companies to invest in proper firearms training for employees. Unfortunately, cases of successful use of firearms by security guards during an incident are incomparably lower than cases of accidental deaths and injuries caused by their incorrect and unsafe use.

What do Security Companies Profit From?

Let us be honest! The goal of business is profit while the product is in most cases only a way to achieve it. Naturally, the vast majority of companies will do almost anything to increase their earnings. That sometimes includes walking on the edge of compliance with laws and regulations, exploiting legal imperfections, and saving on whatever they possibly can, and often beyond that, especially if that seems to be the only way to ensure profitability. We should not forget that a security company is a business like any other. As such, it would be naive to believe that the primary concern of security service providers is security and not profits. The main reason to outsource security is to save cost and logically, the price of service is the main decision criterion. However, most decisions that we make will produce a circular domino effect that might eventually backfire. For instance, our cost saving initiatives will force our partners to save on the quality of products and services that they supply us with which could end up costing us more than our pre-saving setup. Basically, while the cost of security service is already extremely low, in order to gain contracts and beat the competition, security companies are pushed to the very limits of profitability which certainly forces them to be even more creative in finding ways to cut costs and save. Naturally, in most cases, their savings will directly impact the quality of the service that we receive and its performance.

> In many cases, the primary concern of security service providers is their profit and not our security.

HOW ARE SECURITY COMPANIES ABLE TO SURVIVE?

Marketing

First of all, naturally, there is marketing. We can take manned guarding companies as an example. Although there are indeed some good and professional companies out there, in some cases, manned guarding companies are not more than suppliers of unskilled labor whose job description is to simply be present on the client's site. However, unjustly adding the word "security" to the name of the company, upgrading the title "guards" to "officers" and calling this particular service "solution" often does the trick. Basically, the clients do get the feeling that they are purchasing value but are in reality getting even less than what they are paying for, somewhere between almost nothing and very little.

Saving on the Quality

Now that all supporting functions are being outsourced, especially security, private security companies are facing the problem of having to employ staff quickly, in order to meet the headcount requirements of their clients. Moreover, in the time of a global economy crisis, the security industry is experiencing an overload of job applications. Basically, unskilled workers who have lost their jobs owing to cuts and layoffs are often forced to turn to security which is one of the fastest growing industries worldwide, but also an industry that still has quite a loose employment criteria and often very little regulatory oversight. Unfortunately, employment in the private security sector has long been a matter of necessity, not of choice which certainly reflects on the quality of workforce. This overload in demands both by clients and by jobseekers often exceeds the background screening, training, and proper people and process management capacities of security companies. This is especially true for the manned guarding part of security which is the largest piece of the industry. Security companies are forced to employ cheaper unskilled workers and immediately dress them in a uniform. Low pay rates influence job retention, which is somewhere between medium and low.

> The industry of security services often has quite a loose employment criteria and usually very little regulatory oversight.

However, the truth is that quality issues are not to be blamed solely on security companies. Actually, many security companies try to do the best they can to survive with what their clients are willing to pay for the services that they provide. As long as, in commercial enterprises, security is regarded just as a figure and not as a function, it is fairly unlikely that anything will change.

THE MAIN IDEAS BEHIND OUTSOURCING?

Outsourcing is Fashionable

It would be fair to say that outsourcing is a trend. However, like any other trend, it does not necessarily have to be positive or practical in every situation. While the ideas behind security outsourcing hold water in theory, and probably made more practical sense when the trend started, during the years of copy pasting, companies got used to regarding the benefits of outsourcing as a universal truth, with no need to question it and investigate whether these widely accepted benefits actually produce a positive outcome, or if they are even applicable to their specific business model. Commercial enterprises will mostly analyze the profitability and the quality of supplied services and materials only if they directly have a say in the product and the bottom line. However not much time or thought is invested in rethinking and justifying the outsourcing of services that are believed not to directly influence the core business. That certainly does not mean that all outsourcing falls under the Emperor's New Clothes Syndrome. However, it still makes sense to take a deeper look at security outsourcing, reinforce or bust myths and along the way, remind ourselves why we actually need security, what we want from it (accept that it is cheap), what are the results that we expect from it, what is it that we certainly do not want, and how to get it where we want it to be. Of course, should we opt to outsource some of our security services, the success, including its financial dimension, will depend on how thoroughly we assess all the pros and cons; how well we understand the benefits of the service and its influence on the overall business; how well we succeed to tailor the service model to our specific circumstances and needs; and how much time and energy we devote to properly managing processes and controlling performance.

> Many companies don't invest enough time or thought in rethinking and justifying the outsourcing of services that are believed not to directly influence the core business.

Outsourcing Can Save Costs

As much as we can define the period that we live in as the era of information and lack of time, it is also the era of cost saving. Obviously, one of the primary reasons why companies choose to outsource is to lower operational and labor costs. But will outsourcing really lower the costs associated with security? It depends. Basically, the bigger and more complex a security organization is in a company, the more direct financial sense it makes to outsource it. However, the least portion of the saving would be related to the actual workforce. Actually, in some countries, such as in the UK, it is even cheaper to hire in-house security officers that are not required to have a security guard's license than, for instance, hiring a security company that is obligated by law to supply only licensed, more expensive security officers. As for the difference in the quality between licensed and unlicensed security officers, although a license does add certain weight, it is my opinion that it would be naive to rely only on the license. Basically, in many countries, a license only consists of a fee and a basic background check followed by a short course. This type of licensing certainly cannot be regarded as the ultimate proof of skill, competence, and correct mindset. Still, operational costs will mostly benefit from saving on equipment and its maintenance by having the contractor supply regular and specialized security vehicles, X-rays, metal detectors, communication devices, protection equipment, and all the other gear that we would otherwise have to purchase and maintain.

> In reality, the smallest portion of the saving is related to the actual workforce.

Outsourcing Can Lower Production Expenses

Another reason for outsourcing is to be able to reduce and increase the number of security officers in real-time based on our needs. Certainly, in theory, if we outsource, we can easily reduce the number of security guards should we start producing less and rehire them immediately when we start producing more. In this way, our spending on security will follow our revenues. However, this is very different in practice. Apart from the hospitality industry where we might be able to plan and contract security based on the peak season, in most other industries it is often more difficult to accurately predict volume changes. Even if we manage to forecast it, it is very unlikely that our security service provider will accept such an arrangement. Principally, as we would not want to have unutilized employees, our contractor would not want it either. Also, with this arrangement, we would not only spend more time on training and controlling new employees but would also drastically increase the workforce traffic in our company and multiply security risks associated with it, instead of lowering them. Keeping in mind the high percentage of crimes committed by current or ex-security employees, this enormously increases the risk of crimes being committed against us. Finally, even if we would somehow make it work, the truth is that the number of security positions rarely depends on the volume. Basically, in a production plant, the number of gates and entrances, the size of the facility, and the risks will not diminish with lower production. Just like in retail, the number of required security guards will not decrease with the smaller number of articles on the shelves. On the other hand, hiring external agencies occasionally to assist with the security of corporate events or other occasions that call for additional workforce certainly makes sense. However, we can always do it regardless of our regular security setup and weather it is in-house or outsourced.

We Pay Man Hours and Not People

A company must pay salaries to its in-house security officers even when it is not using them, for instance, during vacations and sick leaves. On top of that, it must compensate officers that are their replacements. On the other hand, the company will pay to the provider of security services based on man hours that were actually used. Of course, every position comes with a replacement that can be arranged quickly. This is certainly one of the biggest financial and managerial advantages of outsourcing. However, if we talk about the operational side of having positions and not people, we have to take into account that what we get is usually similar to what we pay for—only attended positions but not always effective people. Basically, in most cases, the replacements that we will receive from the outsourced company will be the ones that are available at that moment, and not necessarily the ones that know anything about our company, its processes, products, culture, location, people, job specifics, threats, and vulnerabilities.

We Can Increase Performance

One more reason is to increase performance by delegating certain supporting processes to external agencies that are believed to be specialists in that particular field. It is true while manned guarding companies account for the biggest part of the security industry, there are numerous specialized professional security companies whose expertise we might require occasionally. Such companies are, for instance, dealing with technical systems (engineering, selling, and installing), security consulting companies, companies that are delivering specialized trainings, private military companies, hostage rescue consultants, investigation agencies, etc. On the contrary, occupational services provided by manned guarding companies in most cases cannot be called specialized. An exception could be the professional security companies that supply armed security guards that we would have to hire to safeguard our operations in hostile, usually foreign, locations.

In any case, the truth is that the level of performance of outsourced security relies on the professional guidance by the in-house security management which is the link between the business goals and security requirements of the company and the fulfillment of these needs by the hired security provider. The quality of the service that we will receive from our service provider will be the mirror image of our concern and involvement in security. Without that, our security would serve more as a presentation, and usually a bad one, than as actual security.

> If our intention is to use security only as a presentation and not as actual
> support, it will simply end up being a bad presentation.

Security is not a core business but every security department is different and the way it works depends on the core business and the knowledge of the staff about core business processes. Security companies provide some sort of general training, but only in the actual place of work can officers really start learning the job, which will require time and money that will not be covered by the security company. Of course, as security companies have a high personnel turnover, this investment is likely to become a loss within a short time.

Another downside is the limited number of tools that we can actually use to increase the performance of outsourced staff and effectively motivate them. It is very difficult to promote unity, ownership, teamwork, and common goals and values if we have an entire department in a company working for another company. In some cases, outsourced employees are even instructed by their companies to keep a low profile in communication with the client. It is also quite a challenge to use the system of reward and punishment to improve the performance of outsourced staff.

When we talk about compensation, it is believed that motivation cannot be increased through salaries; however, that might only be true in the case of increasing salaries to increase motivation. In the case when salaries are becoming lower such as during takeover of in-house security staff by a contractor, the salary issue will definitely have a negative impact on employee motivation and consequently on performance. It is naive to believe that a drastic difference between salaries of staff employed directly and outsourced staff will not have an impact on motivation and ownership. Even in case of an agreement between the company and a service provider to keep the salaries as they were, because of the added company fees, the deal would probably end up being more expensive. Finally, that kind of deal would have to have an expiry date and would eventually become an issue.

> The opinion that motivation cannot be influenced with salaries might only be
> true in cases when salaries are increasing.

Outsourcing Allows Us to Focus on Core Business

Companies also choose to outsource so that they may continue focusing on their core business processes while delegating dull time consuming processes to external agencies. Well, one of the main points of this book is to actually prove that security is a core business process. We are often so accustomed to regarding security as a support process that we often fail to see that in our specific industry it could be the vital ingredient of the product and, as such, a core business function. For example, in the industry of financial services, travel industry, or hospitality, security does not only protect the business but also shapes the product, influences customers' opinions, and eventually sells. However, also in other industries, the importance of security in consumers' behavior and decisions is rapidly growing. Basically, instead of going with the "we have always done it this way" justification for outsourcing security, we should first determine to what extent security is really vital for our business and what are the direct and indirect benefits that we get from it. We have to analyze all the performance upsides as a result of managing security directly and matching it with the specific needs of our business and the financial downsides of keeping it in-house. Moreover, before deciding to outsource, we have to be sure that the direct financial benefits of outsourcing will be greater than the overall functional and financial benefits of regarding security as a crucial process, keeping it in-house and managing it closely.

We Outsource Responsibility

By delegating responsibilities to external agencies companies can legally wash their hands off functions that are difficult to manage and control while still realizing their benefits. However, we often falsely believe that by outsourcing legal responsibility, we are also minimizing the possibility of tangible and reputational risks or their consequences. Actually, when we outsource responsibility, we usually, naturally, completely remove the outsourced service from our focus. One of the most common mistakes that we make when thinking about risk and responsibility is to regard them as just two different names for one concept and confusing the outsourcing of responsibility with the mitigation of risks.

> We often confuse outsourcing of responsibility with mitigation of risks.

Certainly, the Service Agreement itself will not increase our security. In case of a failure of our security service providers during an incident, the legal responsibility might be theirs, together with the financial responsibility for direct losses. However, we would first have to prove that they are indeed legally responsible for the loss which can be quite challenging. Basically, the limited number of scenarios that we can predict and insert in our Service Agreement is no match for the unlimited number of unpredicted situations that could actually occur which might not fall under the legal responsibility of the contracted company. Finally, even if we would manage to be reimbursed for the direct damages, the usually more severe indirect damages such as damaged reputation and shaken client confidence would remain. We have to remember that, by outsourcing responsibility, we are putting our own reputation in someone else's hands. We should also know that with responsibility, we are also outsourcing performance and control. Moreover, this outsourced control is not only functional control but also financial control as we are also tied to the financial well-being of our service provider which could go bankrupt and leave us holding the bag.

Case Study: Outsourcing the Responsibility for the Organization of Marketing Events

A good example for the outsourcing of responsibility is the marketing events that are part of the marketing strategy of a famous international beer manufacturer. The company promotes its brands, especially the company's main brand, through party-like massive music events. In order to limit possible legal issues, the company hands over the official organization and management of its events to service providers while it legally appears only as the sponsor of these events. The outsourced companies are responsible for organizing all the elements of events, including logistics, safety, and security. On the other hand, the beer manufacturer feels that it is not obligated to be involved in the outsourced processes, apart from branding, which is anyway the main purpose of venues. Naturally, all the security and safety flaws would be the legal responsibility of the outsourced company which is the official organizer. Still, we have to remember that if the event is turning around a specific brand, apart from legal issues that would be covered, in case of reputational issues, it would be the reputation of the brand that would suffer the consequences, and not the reputation of a no-name service provider. Moreover, the damages to the reputation of the brand would end up being much costlier than any penalties. It is, therefore, much smarter to take the faith of our brand in our own hands, even if we do officially outsource certain aspects of the performance of events. For this particular brand, there are numerous known cases of safety negligence during events, such as equipment not being properly mounted and power installations that are not properly secured that resulted in injuries. Also, there are continuous security flaws such as minors being allowed to enter the venues, use of illegal narcotics, violence, and other incidents. While it is indeed the service providers that are suffering the legal consequences, it is the actual brand that is getting negative publicity, instead of profiting from exposure.

WHAT TO AVOID WHEN OUTSOURCING SECURITY

Outsourcing the Management

Security is not a concept that can exist without being given a framework and being placed in a context ("Security of..." and "Protection from..."). Basically, in commercial enterprises, in order to make sense, security has to be applied to the specific circumstances and goals of the business. Certainly, the biggest mistake in outsourcing is handing over the management of outsourced service to the service provider. As security needs a framework, all its elements have to be coordinated in order to jointly provide a solution and serve their purpose. For instance, Manned Guarding is not a standalone system but part of the overall security system of the company that also includes Information, Management, Communication, Technology, Physical Parameters, and Procedures. Basically, the purpose of security management is to unite all the elements of a security system in order to produce and maintain a successful security organization that is a partner to the specific business and as such able to address all the specific challenges that a company is facing or might face in the future. As we have mentioned earlier, the fact that our service providers call a particular service "solution" does not mean that they actually have the capacity to ensure the overall protection of our business.

In order to be able to manage our security efficiently, private security companies would have to completely understand our company, its culture, its products, and its customers. They would have to be well-informed, understand the impact that the global and local climate, such as politics and economy, can have on our security, be able to process data, predict events, and implement timely adjustments by combining physical and technical security, develop procedures, perform trainings, and collect and protect information and developing communication channels. Certainly, they would also require direct access to the top management of the company in order to be able to influence the business and be influenced by it. Unfortunately, most private security companies are based on day-to-day service and are mainly concentrated on routine activities and emergency response without spending resources and energy on understanding the causes and observing trends, predicting unfavorable developments, and adjusting accordingly. Of course, according to the employment criteria mentioned previously, it would be unrealistic to expect it. The reality is that private security companies' managements often do not even seem interested in learning the specifics of the business to which they are providing a service to.

Using More Companies for One Service

Some companies prefer to have several service providers for one service. Sometimes, we will indeed have to use more service providers for different security services, such as Consulting, Technology, Training, or Investigations. Also, in case of a multi-market structure enterprise with parallel structures for each market, we will not necessarily use one international provider of security services but the company that would be the best in satisfying our needs in the specific market. Also, if our processes differ from market to market, or we have a complex operation in one market, we might not be able to find a security provider that would be able to cover such a broad spectrum of services but would have to contract several companies. For instance, if in one market we would have a Production Plant, Supply Chain, Headquarters, Expatriates, and a Retail Network, we would require Manned Guarding, Supply Chain Security, Cash in Transit, Retail Loss Prevention, and Executive Protection. However, some companies chose to split one process between several providers by, for example, using two or more manned guarding companies, even in one homogenous geographical area. One of the main reasons for such a direction is to ensure business continuity. Basically, in case of performance issues with one of the outsourced companies, other service providers that already know the work and have experience with our company would be easily able to take over. Another reason is not to give one service provider complete power and control over an entire process, which would eventually make it more difficult to replace that particular company. While this concern does make sense, by having in-house security management that is directly involved in designing, managing, and controlling the processes, that risk would be minimal. Companies also often believe that, by using several service providers, they would raise the quality of service through competition. While this may seem logical in theory, in practice, it usually comes down to companies wasting time on accusations and trying to prove that their competition is wrong and incompetent instead of using that energy to improve their performance. Basically, having multiple security service providers adds unnecessary complexity and makes security management more difficult and less controllable which reflects on its overall quality. Finally, it will usually end up being more expensive.

> Using more security service providers for one service makes the process less controllable and its management more difficult.

Making Our Service Providers Our Clients

Although this rule should not require additional explaining, I have witnessed numerous cases where service providers were also business clients of the company that they are working for. Business naturally has the impulse to sell. However, our service providers should be excluded from the Always Be Selling (ABS) principle. By this, I certainly do not mean that service providers should not be allowed to purchase our products on the free marker, or even be encouraged to do so. Also, there is no reason not to offer discounted prices to our partners. On the other hand, we must never fall into the trap of going into a deal with the outsourced company that would require continuing to hire that particular company in order not to lose money. For instance, there are no rare cases that banks require from their service providers to become their clients that can then apply for all the other services, such as loans and mortgages. There are also many cases when the initial deal between a bank and a service provider includes bank loans to the hired company to, for instance, purchase equipment that is required to secure the bank. Moreover, the only assurance for the loan is often the service contract itself. Basically, this means that we would have to continue to hire the particular service provider in order to make sure that the loan would be payed back. The same goes for, for example, car manufacturers that would grant loans to their service provider for purchasing vehicles which would be payed from the service compensation.

Case Study: Bank Loans to Service Providers

A big international bank is the perfect example of how not to manage service providers. In one of the markets, in order to show good business results, prior to signing service agreements, the bank required from all the external companies, including its security service provider, to become corporate clients of the bank and to refinance their dues to other banks and even take new loans. After the initial service period, on the following tenders, the bank was forced to rehire the same security service provider even after severe performance flaws, and although the particular company was far from submitting the lowest bid or giving the best conditions, simply so that they could assure the return of the loans. Actually, the fact that the outsourced company had to rely on that particular contract to pay off the loans, which should have been a sign of financial trouble and a red alert for the bank in the first place, resulted in the company not being able to perform the services that it was contracted to perform, or to even compensate its employees. The employees that were not paid vastly abandoned their workplaces, while some, apart from suing their company, also filed lawsuits against the bank. Many employees also turned to the media which caused extremely bad press. In some branches, employees that were looking up to the bank to solve the situation organized strikes in order to convince the bank to take action and force their direct employer to pay them the missing salaries. On the other hand, the local management of the bank continued to use the services of the particular company in order to cover-up the bad decision that they have made at the beginning and hide the consequences from the headquarters. Finally, the deal ended up being stripped of practically any performance and still much more expensive than an in-house security organization would have been. It also required additional time, energy, and resources to try to fix, or at least, mask the flaws. The deal also produced bad financial results and severely damaged the reputation of the bank.

CHOOSING A PROVIDER OF MANNED GUARDING SERVICES

The company has chosen the option of not burdening the core business with the organization of security services within the company, wants to lower security related expenses, or the existing security service does not work the way in which it is expected. The company searches for a security provider that will respond to all requests and needs in the field of security while confirming the financial justification of the whole project.

Open Sources

The first step toward introducing security companies operating in the market can be to search an open source (Internet, media, etc.), ask for a recommendation from someone who had experience with a similar project, or open a public announcement of procurement. In all three cases, it is likely that the choice will be wrong. Searching for a security provider through an open source such as the Internet will result in a large quantity of mostly useless and even false information. It is common for companies to advertise enormous staff capacity, knowledge, experience, and state-of-the-art equipment and to list hundreds of respectful clients and then prove to be no more than one-man-show companies with no real abilities. Moreover, tens and sometimes even hundreds of companies call themselves market leaders.

Recommendations

First-hand recommendations can be the basis for selecting a service provider. However, security risks, threats, and consequently security needs vary not only within different industries, but also within the same industry and similar processes. Depending on the micro-locations, social circumstances, the complexity of facilities, and so forth, a successful security provider in one company can prove to be a completely wrong choice for another company. For instance, in addition to capacity and professional capabilities, a security service provider must have sufficient presence (for example, staff, technology, and infrastructure) in the specific geographical area to respond in a timely and successful manner to incidents and special requests. A large respectful security company will be useless if it has no significant operations in the required location. Another aspect is the level of attention the security service provider gives to its clients. Large companies certainly have a higher potential to respond to the needs of their clients. However, large companies with numerous clients might not be able to devote the same level of attention to all of their clients, but will, mostly based on profit (and not on the level of risk), classify clients into categories, and certainly take more care of their key accounts than other companies which they regard as less important. Sometimes, choosing a smaller service provider will generate better result in terms of care, attention, and response time.

Public Procurement

Open public advertising of procurement is usually a waste of valuable time because of the numerous companies that apply for it. In many cases, companies will apply even if they do not meet the required criteria. Worse, some companies will even provide false information regardless of the consequences.

Search Criteria

Companies should definitely look for a security provider that offers a broad range of multiple security services and has a capacity beyond immediate requirements. Like when hiring new employees, references are important. A company should definitely contact them for feedback. A good sign for service providers could be high customer retention and customers who have extended their contracts multiple times. This gives some level of quality assurance that the security service provider can really deliver. The advantage should be given to a security provider who is profitable and reinvests most profits back into growing its operational capabilities. However, finding a profitable security service provider could prove to be challenging with so many security service providers that depend on constant venture capital. Security officers are often the weakest link in the security company. Knowing that the staff has relevant capabilities, training, and security clearances and that these criteria are taken into account during the recruitment process is important. A security service provider should have experience in the particular industry and assign staff who are experienced in specific environments and in performing specific tasks. Expectations and penalties should be well-defined and clearly stated in the service agreement. For the expectations to be met and flaws sanctioned, the entire process should be described in detail, as well as time frames within which the company can expect a response.

> We should search for a security provider who is profitable and reinvests most profits back into growing its operational capabilities.

CHAPTER SUMMARY

Outsourcing is not just another name for cost saving. Basically, in some industries and when applied to certain business models, security outsourcing might produce good financial results. However, in some circumstances, not only that it would not be directly financially sound, but could even indirectly cause great harm to the company, its core processes, and profits. For instance, in the hospitality industry, security is not only a vital part of the product but is becoming one of the key criteria of clients and an important marketing and sales tool. Moreover, the complexity of the hospitality industry requires security to be both a performance and a presentation. While outsourcing in order to save costs might produce direct savings, handing over the control of the performance and presentation of one of our key elements to a contractor might prove to be a bad decision in the long run. Actually, it is exactly managing security as a core process, maintain close control, and investing in it that might stimulate profits that could prove to be more beneficial on all levels than any direct savings could have been.

Furthermore, even when we assess the benefits of outsourcing, we usually only look at our needs and start investigating possible contractors only once a decision to outsource has been made. For example, in the centralized model of corporate governance, it is not rare that company's headquarters make unified decisions for all the markets without taking their specific circumstances into account. While we might even choose the best company in the market, that does not necessarily mean that the market best would be good enough. Basically, like in any marriage, the success of outsourcing does not only depend on one side but on the individual quality of all sides and, more importantly, their interaction. Clearly, apart from looking at the entire business when investigating the pros and cons of outsourcing, the decision process if to outsource or not should involve a detailed investigation of the market to determine if there are indeed contractors that could provide the specific service that we are planning to outsource and supply the quality that we require.

Certainly, we can make outsourcing successful, both in terms of operational and financial benefits only if we understand what we really need and what an external provider of security services can actually supply. If we can have a service provider that provides workforce that we handpick, if we have mechanisms to influence job retention, if we can train outsourced employees and match them to our needs, and if we can influence performance, closely manage, direct and control the outsourced organization, outsourcing could produce satisfactory results. Together with that, we would not waste valuable time and funds on purchasing and maintaining necessary security equipment and personal gear. However, finding a suitable service provider and having a favorable arrangement would certainly be a challenge, to say the least.

SELF-ASSESSMENT/DISCUSSION QUESTIONS

1. How much time and effort does your company invest in assessing the pros and cons prior to outsourcing supporting services?

2. What would be your company's main reason for outsourcing manned guarding services?
3. Are you confident with the level of skill, ownership, and overall performance of the outsourced manned guarding staff in your company?
4. Do you think that the management of the external service provider understands your company, its culture, products, specific risks, and vulnerabilities?
5. Would you rate the benefit that you get from a service provider as equal to price?
6. Is your service provider able to contribute to your company's core processes, influence the leadership of the company, and follow their directions?
7. Do you believe that you successfully outsource risks by outsourcing responsibility?
8. On what abilities and features do you base your requirements when searching for a suitable security service provider?
9. Do you believe that you have complete control over outsourced processes and employees that perform them?

SECTION

IV

Utilize

CHAPTER 10

Resilience: The Wider Concept of Security

THE FINANCIAL SIGNIFICANCE OF RESILIENCE

Risk is often defined as the "effect of uncertainty on objectives." Actually, some of the most challenging business tasks are connected to risk as it is closely related to profit and greatly influences it. This includes understanding and forecasting risks, determining our risk appetite and its boundaries, and having mechanisms that will minimize it and limit its consequences. In today's world, with the increase in the frequency, speed, and severity of threats, it is unavoidable that our business will be impacted and will be forced to fight severe challenges and quickly recover from incidents in order to survive. Logically, our profit and even our existence depend on how well we deal with risks. Certainly, risk is a complex phenomenon that includes numerous dimensions that always accompany each other. However, whether we are assessing the risks of investing in a financially turbulent market, or the risk of default on our loans, they are always accompanied by security threats. Actually, security threats are probably the biggest influencers of all other risks and security incidents are often the first signs of financial instabilities. Unfortunately, the reality is that in most commercial organizations, various functions that are dealing with different aspects of risks, rarely cooperate or even communicate, let alone having the entire organization united in noticing and addressing hazards and recovering from incidents. While Risk Management can be defined as "coordinated activities that are intended to direct and control an organization with regard to risk," it is Organizational Resilience that unites all the elements of an organization around that goal without relying exclusively on security and other risk management functions. Regardless of whether we understand resilience as a security concept, financial concept, or both, the truth is that by investing our efforts in making a compact organization with all its elements working closer to each other in addressing security threats, we will certainly benefit on all levels.

From Corporate Security to Commercial Force. DOI: http://dx.doi.org/10.1016/B978-0-12-805149-8.00010-8

GOOD SECURITY DOES NOT NECESSARILY MEAN GOOD RESILIENCE

While it was once believed that organizational resilience should be naturally performed by security, or security related functions in an enterprise, the truth is that these functions are just one step in the overall resilience of an organization. As I am primarily a security practitioner with a military and homeland security background, it would be logical to assume that I would mostly consult on, and write about "hands-on" security, such as terrorism, physical security tactics, or security technology. Instead, I often write about the application of security in a business scenery and all the accompanying hardships, challenges, and missed opportunities. So, instead of addressing only the threats, like crime and terrorism and security tactics against them, I like to analyze corporate security through the wider concept of organizational security resilience. The reason for it is quite simple. We would not assess the overall success of the security system of an organization based on identified threats and the measures that it is implementing against them but based on its overall success in overcoming security challenges. We often fail to understand that resilience is not the natural outcome of good security practices but that it is actually the result of the overall organizational understanding of security and risks, support from the stakeholders, and their commitment to really address vulnerabilities. If we were to compare building resilience to building a wall, security actions would be the bricks while support from the stakeholders would be the cement that holds them together. So, as much as teamwork does not rely only on the individual qualities of the team members, we cannot produce results by relying only on the independent, job specific qualities of functions in an enterprise but on the quality of their interaction. Basically, piles of bricks and buckets of cement will not build a wall unless they interact.

> Security functions are just one step in the overall resilience of an organization.

The Difference Between Security and Resilience

I have seen numerous examples of bad security resilience in successful enterprises where both security and core business processes are managed and executed by professionals that are outstanding in their fields of expertise. Moreover, business leaders have a clear vision concerning business goals and strategies while security managers effectively identify risks and address vulnerabilities, and still, the resilience of the organization is substandard. However, to make it clearer, we should first explain what is security, what is resilience, what are the differences, and what are the meeting points. Simply put,

Security is a process of risks reduction, while Resilience is the flexibility of an entity and its ability to adapt to changing security conditions, recover from failures, and learn lessons.

> Resilience requires flexibility to adapt to changing security conditions,
> recover from failures and learn lessons.

If we take hotels as an example, we could rate the security of a hotel as better or worse based on the measures that it is implementing and their success. On the other hand, the hospitality industry in general has completely failed when it comes to resilience by refusing to accept the new security reality, understand that it has become the primary target of terrorism, recognize the shifting priorities of their guests, and adapt.

In retail organizations, in my opinion, the concept of Loss Prevention including the title itself shows the lack of security flexibility. Basically, while Loss Prevention should certainly be one of the most important aspects of the security of retail, in many retail organizations it is the function that is responsible for designing and managing all the security efforts of the organization. Principally, the philosophy, required competences, job descriptions, set-up and usually the entire retail security attitude focuses only on preventing direct losses. Practically, the role of loss prevention is to control what goes out of the site and we can rate the security of a store according to its success in meeting that target. However, the growing complexity of risks requires from retail organizations to expend the competences of their security also to what/who comes in. So, even when we talk about financial losses, weapons, explosives, or poison that are brought into a supermarket will certainly cause more direct and indirect losses than anything that was stolen from it.

Misconceptions About Resilience

The general understanding of resilience is that it is a system that should simply limit the consequences of events which actually equalizes it with Business Continuity Management (BCM). However, I believe that an overall concept such as resilience, that should be flexible in mitigating risks, should not be simply defined. Basically, every attempt to define a concept makes it stiffer and takes away from its potential to be truly elastic. That is mostly why I prefer to explain resilience as loosely and as widely as possible. Moreover, for me, resilience is far more than just remedy. It is a perception and a system that includes a global mindset in understanding threats and adapting to changing security conditions. It is the ability of an organization to notice and prevent risks at the earliest possible stage without exclusively relying on the security department. It is also the ability of organization to isolate the effects of an incident and prevent them from spreading further, as well as to successfully recover from it.

Understanding the Concept of Vulnerability as the First Step in Embracing Resilience

We usually understand incidents as isolated harmful events. Consequently, we conceptualize vulnerability as inability to protect from these events. As a result, we wrongly visualize protection as a shield around an organization and not as an interconnected system of barriers throughout the organization. However, by looking at incidents as isolated events and not as phenomena that continue to impact the business and cost money even after they have seemingly ended, we are failing to see the depth of incidents and their long-lasting economic influence. The truth is that most of the novelty business philosophies that are aimed at saving costs and increasing productivity left resilience behind as collateral damage. For example, by embracing the "Just-in-Time" (JIT) principle, we succeeded to lower the costs of production and avoid building stock. Naturally, JIT requires flawless frequent supply of raw materials that are required for production. When we assess our vulnerabilities, we will certainly identify the theft of raw materials in supply chain as a probability and analyze our preparedness to prevent it. Unfortunately, we will usually not take into account the effect that this incident will have on the production and the arrival of the product to consumers. Even when we have business continuity plans that should assure undisrupted production it will usually not be part of an overall strategy but a standalone action in one part of the lifecycle of the product. Basically, security will address the incident without trying to understand its consequences while BCM will address the consequences without paying attention to the cause. However, we would not be able to learn lessons and exercise flexibility without aligning strategies and working together toward common goals.

> We understand protection as an external shield and not as an interconnected system of internal barriers.

We could take Information Security as the perfect example that could further illustrate the lack of resilience as a result of managing parts of processes as separate functions instead of understanding them and managing them as overall concepts. Actually, the famous dilemma if stolen flash memory that contains sensitive information is the responsibility of ICT Security or Physical Security exactly demonstrates our misconception that security is a function and not a concept. Furthermore, the division of responsibilities between the traditional security and ICT security increased the vulnerability of information. Basically, while the security department sees ICT security as the function that is responsible for the security of information, ICT security is usually only concerned with electronic information and regards it as purely technological and not as a phenomenon that exists regardless of the form, or the media that contains it.

ORIGIN AND DIRECTION OF RESILIENCE

Although security and resilience certainly do influence each other, they are far from being the same. In commercial organizations, a big difference between security and resilience is also their origin and their direction. Security is practically exercised at the hierarchical bottom of the organization and spreads outwards, while resilience originates at the top of the enterprise and speeds inwards. In banks, for instance, physical security is conceptually managed by the security function while it is practically performed by security officers and clerks in branches where the bank interacts with its clients and functions as a line of defense. Regardless of the strategic vision of the security management, the actual practical abilities of physical security do not reach far beyond noticing and mitigating immediate threats such as crime, fraud, or ongoing attack. Moreover, security measures are designed to address only the identified probable risks. However, corporate security alone often does not have the solutions for incidents that have managed to pass the first line of defense or in case of unexpected immediate risks, unless the entire organization is united and determined to identify them and address them. Resilience on the other hand is initiated by the leadership that spreads it through the entire organization. We can also look at security resilience as practically exercised security culture of an organization.

Resilience is the outcome of the security culture of an organization.

SECURITY AND RESILIENCE ON THE EXAMPLE OF HOMELAND SECURITY

One way of explaining the difference between security and resilience would be on the example of Homeland Security in Western Europe, especially in France, Belgium, and Germany in the period between 2014 and 2016. We can assume that homeland security organizations of most western countries have similar abilities when it comes to tracking, preventing, and combating terrorism. Basically, the close cooperation between countries, such as sharing of knowledge and intelligence and creating joint strategies, pretty much erased the differences in the quality of security agencies in different countries that once existed. Still, the successes of terrorist attacks that recently occurred in Europe are indicators of inadequate resilience rather than being the result of security agencies failures. Basically, some countries were too slow in adapting to changing security conditions. Firstly, political decisions and security strategies were not coordinated sufficiently. For instance, domestic security tactics did not follow important developments with the potential to severely alter the security climate, such as the involvement of military in the Middle East or the Europe Migrant Crisis. Second, the cooperation and coordination between state security services and private security sectors can be in the least classified as substandard. Also, security collaboration between homeland security agencies and the corporate sector barely exists. For example, during this time of overwhelming terrorist threats, there are hardly any nationwide strategies and official security standards that companies have to obey, as they are, for instance, required to comply with Environment, Health, and Safety regulations. Businesses are completely free to decide if they are going to have any security at all, and if they do, they can arrange it according to their judgement. Finally, citizens' security awareness in Europe is only now starting to improve. Unfortunately, it is being built the hard way, as outcome of tragedies, and not as result of the correct preventive approach.

> Businesses are often misusing the freedom to decide if they are going to have security and the liberty to arrange it per their own judgement.

RESILIENCE VERSUS BUSINESS CONTINUITY AND DISASTER RECOVERY

Businesses often confuse organizational Resilience with Business Continuity Management and Disaster Recovery (BCM & DR). Business Continuity is a management process that identifies potential impacts that threaten an organization and provides a framework for an effective response to safeguard the interests of its key stakeholders, reputation, brand, and value-creating activities. It identifies the risk of exposure of business processes to internal and external threats, quantifies and mitigates their impact, and ensures fast and efficient recovery in case of a disaster.

The Limits of BCM & DR

As much as we want to believe the BCM & DR has the influence, reach, required flexibility and potential to effectively protect a company from disruptions, this is not its purpose and certainly not its ability. The truth is that BCM & DR is actually a stiff system that is performed on a management level with only very limited and shallow involvement of regular workforce. First of all, its primary purpose is not to prevent incidents but to prevent incidents from becoming disasters and to prevent disasters from becoming tragedies. BCM & DR is also mostly not concerned with the nature of incidents but mostly with their consequences, which makes it quite useless when it comes to protecting an organization from security risks. BCM & DR does anticipate some disruptions but that is mostly limited to recurring happenings such as natural disasters or infrastructure failures that are typical for certain seasons or areas. For instance, we basically know what natural risks exist and which are associated with what part of the year. We relatively accurately know when to expect heat waves, floods, or epidemics, and based on that knowledge, we can create an effective template for business continuity plans and disaster recovery. We also know that cell phone networks overload during holidays and that increased numbers of cyberattacks occur during certain holidays. Unfortunately, in practice, business continuity and disaster recovery is a topic that is related almost exclusively to ICT services that support the organization's critical business activities. A proper business continuity plan usually also accounts for events that are not disastrous but may cause business disruption, such as the unavailability of the critical minimum number of employees, for instance, in the vacation season or during important religious holidays.

> BCM & DR is mostly not concerned with the nature of incidents but mostly with their consequences, which makes it quite useless when it comes to protecting an organization from security risks.

While BCM & DR is certainly one of the very important tools aimed at strengthening the resilience of an organization, the two are far from being equal. Resilience is actually a wider concept with a deeper reach in which BCM plays a role.

BUILDING ORGANIZATIONAL SECURITY RESILIENCE

So, how do we build resilience? Resilience requires that all core and support functions understand both security and risks and their impact on the business and on the clients, as well as the role that they should play in mitigating those risks. Resilience requires that security leadership has the knowledge and the mandate to design, implement and manage security, that organizational leadership understands, supports and encourages security, and emphasizes it as an important part of the organizational culture, and that employees are willing and able to actively participate in it. Basically, while the security of a facility relies on the 5D1R principle (Deter, Detect, Deny, Delay, Defend, and Recover), the resilience of an organization works according to the same concept but with different means, on a much larger scale, and with an entire organization united and working together.

Preparing for Both Probability and Possibility

As we have already mentioned, Resilience is a wider concept than both Security and BCM & DR. It is about how an organization responds to changes. Certainly the most successful strategy of responding to change would be to anticipate it and specifically prepare for it. However, changes are changing in a way that we cannot predict them as efficiently as we could have in the past which certainly makes it harder to prepare. No one can predict with certainty when and how a serious disruption to business will occur. The business continuity of an organization can be affected in many ways. Severe security incidents, natural disasters that destroy the premises and property and stop the business, extreme weather conditions that disrupt the supply chain, pollution of water required for production, product recalls, epidemics, power cuts, and the failure of critical ICT systems and applications are just some examples of events that can affect organizations, causing business discontinuity and costing millions, and sometimes even billions.

We typically combine two models of strategies when building resilience. First, as every member of an institution is responsible for security on some level, we try to anticipate as many possible disruptions, and plan the role of each position in the organization in noticing probable threats, mitigating risks and recovering from incidents. We require access to important information and a proper system of processing them and turning them into strategies. Having information is absolutely essential for a security system to be able to survive. Just as a living organism continuously searches for new sources of food and water by using its brain, senses, and strength, a security system uses all of its elements to collect and process information. It simply starts with being well informed about any global and local developments that could affect our security. Certainly, being informed also requires good working relationship with the law enforcement, being active in security forums, and using common sense when making a link between, for instance, political and economic influencers and their possible security outcome. Still, as risks do not only originate from outside the organization but also from inside, having an efficient mechanism that can capture relevant internal information is absolutely crucial. However, as we mostly base tactics on probability and not on possibility, there is an unlimited number of possible threats that we are not specifically prepared for. Certainly, as Resilience requires flexibility, the second model of resilience strategy should be flexible enough to provide the optimal solution for unexpected situations. This is the part where Resilience really steps-in This model of resilience mostly relies on ownership and awareness of all the people in the organization, common sense and logic to notice the unusual, training, knowing and understanding everyone's role during emergencies, effective and timely communication, and emergency leadership that has the ability and the mandate to make quick and reasonable decisions.

> As we mostly base tactics on probability and not on possibility, there is an unlimited number of possible threats that we are not specifically prepared for.

RESILIENCE IS ABOUT PEOPLE

As we have mentioned earlier, the most important features of resilience are flexibility and adaptability. Out of all the elements that form a security system, only people possess the ability to be flexible so that they could adjust all the other elements of security accordingly. So, as much as the core of security is professional expertise, the key element of resilience is people and their willingness to be an active part of the security of an organization. Consequently, the key question would be how to get people to be part of the resilience of an organization. We often hear that getting people to cooperate comes down to helping them understand an issue and its importance so that they could personally relate to it. However, by only explaining, we leave it to each employee to establish an isolated personal connection with security and execute tasks according to his/her personal judgement and logic, or the lack of it. That is certainly not a way to build resilience which actually requires a coordinated team effort.

> Only people possess the ability to be flexible.

Governance

Security governance is an internal framework with which an organization proactively addresses security issues by systematically arranging and explaining the roles, responsibilities, and actions of all its elements and their coordination. Governance is a system of principles, rules, standards, policies, procedures, technical instructions, and working instructions. Basically, in order to arrange and present the role of all the employees in a company as official strategy, we have to publish it in our policies and procedures. Governance is an important tool in building resilience. As such, it is important that we have an efficient governance system, from the top of the governance pyramid and all the way to its bottom. Many organizations are changing their model of governance from a strict Centralized System to a looser Federal Model of Governance. Basically, instead of imposing turnkey policies that might not be completely applicable to a variety of local conditions, companies are realizing that it would be more effective to create general rules or standards and allow their affiliates to create more usable local policies, procedures, and working instructions based on these standards.

Procedures are a crucial element of a security system in every organization. Procedures standardize the actions and responsibilities of the human element of security in combination with technology and physical and mechanical security elements, and regulate routine and emergency communication, management, and proper handling of information. Actually, procedures will greatly influence the mindset of employees and whether they will perceive their security role as additional burden or as part of their regular activities. When regulating the involvement of people in the security system of an organization, we can create special security procedures that accompany every business process. However, in this way we would have many security procedures for each position which would end up being too lengthy to be convenient and effective. A much more effective way to regulate the security efforts of non-security staff is to include a Security Clause in each Standard Procedure thus making it an integral part of regular processes. For example, in the hotel industry, a Front Desk "Guest Luggage Handling Procedure" would include a security clause on how to recognize suspicious marks on luggage and how to handle it safely. However, every company also needs to have special detailed standalone procedures for emergence response such as reaction to emergency situations, crisis management, and disaster recovery. Typically, Security Clauses should contain detailed information on routine security awareness as well as alertness to specific risks that accompany particular process, proper reaction to issues, effective communication, chain of command, as well as necessary actions and desired behavior during issues and incidents that were not anticipated and were not specifically addressed in the procedure.

> Having special security procedures for every business process, would end up being too lengthy to be convenient and effective.

Classification of Positions

Communication, trainings, and basically every information flow requires that you know which horizontal and vertical groups of people exist in your organization and exactly what will be communicated to whom, as well as what level of training is suitable for which group. Resilience requires diversity but, in order to use it to our advantage, we must classify the positions in a way that we will be able to address potential problems from all sides and that all specific actions that should be performed by employees are correctly allocated so that they together form an effective system.

Bank of Talents

Apart from classifying positions, we have to understand that most people have specific talents and abilities that are not necessarily related to their functions and work duties. However, these talents, whether they are technical abilities or personal characteristics, can be enormously helpful for solving problems. Logically, knowing and utilizing the other side of our employees could prove to be beneficial for a business on many levels and not only from the side of our security resilience.

> Knowing the talents of our employees that are not necessarily related to their functions could prove to be beneficial for a business on many levels.

Communication

Effective resilience relies on balanced information and effective communication. Not providing enough vital information is as bad as providing too much. Also, effective communication requires planning who is going to receive what amount and what level of information, but also finding the most effective way to communicate. We could say that communication is the twin of information. Still, although we want all the people to be able to communicate and report issues, we will not be able to use the same communication means. For instance, a production floor employee will probably not have an official e-mail address or a company-issued cell phone. The same goes for housekeeping staff in a hotel. However, it is exactly those positions that could be crucial for security resilience as they are typically the first ones that will notice an issue. Of course, their ability to effectively report the issue will often make a difference between an issue and a disaster. Timely communication is certainly the precondition for timely response.

Training

Every member of an institution is responsible for security on some level. Whereas some employees have more direct responsibility than others, everyone requires training. Basically, not all training subjects are for everyone. Also, different functional groups of employees require different levels of knowledge on the same subject. A thorough and well thought off Training Matrix is an important part of our Resilience strategy.

Personal Example

We have said that Resilience is about people. This rule applies to all the people in an organization, starting from the hierarchical top of the organization and ending at its bottom. To motivate people, the precondition for your message to be taken seriously and perceived as a desirable model of behavior is that you are an example. A good personal image (and thus a good example) is achieved through zealously obeying your own rules. It also requires visible personal commitment, devotion, belief, and integrity.

Reward and Punishment

One of the most successful tools aimed at increasing performance is the system of rewards and punishments. Basically, by rewarding the correct mindset and sanctioning negligence, we do not only create a personal connection of employees with the concept that we support but, more importantly, emphasize the importance that the concept has for us and for our company.

> Rewards and punishments emphasize the importance of security for our company.

Drills and Exercises

During both emergencies and routine, people tend to react in a way with which they are familiar. It is essential to conduct trainings, drills, and exercises to make sure that all people in an organization will do their part to prevent an incident, react to it, and mitigate its impact on themselves and the organization.

GLOBAL UNDERSTANDING OF RISK

One of the most important preconditions of Resilience is to change the way we understand the concept of Risk and how we handle it. As long as we do not see Risk as one concept that can be approached from many angles, we cannot build effective resilience. Basically, as much as the role of security is to mitigate security threats, organizational resilience is the remedy against risks in general. Although we like to divide risks according to their type, such as financial risks and security risks, the truth is that all types of risks have a security side and that they all eventually turn up to be very financial. By splitting risks into categories, we make it harder for ourselves to approach them and handle them effectively as all-round phenomenon, which increases our vulnerabilities to risks and weakens our overall resilience.

THE INFLUENCE OF RESILIENCE ON IMPROVING PRODUCTIVITY

Logically, in order for security to become a commercial force, it takes the entire organization to understand security and resilience and the positive impact that it may have on core processes, products, clients, and the bottom line. The main reason why we do not often use security as a tool in, for instance, marketing and sales is that we simply did not think about it. Resilience as a systematic mindset brings security closer to functions that are usually completely unaware of its philosophies and benefits but could actually use it to greatly improve their own processes and also help security with their activities. Also, as we have mentioned earlier, one of the most important tools of resilience is communication. By encouraging communication that we want to use to increase the resilience of our organization, we also create communication channels, either horizontal or vertical, that will facilitate other business actions. Basically, in large entities, there are functions that do not often have a chance to cooperate in their routine activities as their core processes rarely overlap. Still, by bringing functions closer to each other around a certain agenda, we will increase the possibility of these functions to build closer working relations and to also start to cooperate on other projects. Also, by encouraging flexibility, common sense and logic, and presenting them as important qualities we increase creativity, not only in handling risks but in executing core processes.

> Resilience brings security closer to functions that could use security to improve their own processes.

CHAPTER SUMMARY

For a commercial enterprise, devoting time and efforts into systematically building organizational Resilience will probably be one of the most rewarding investments as it will, with minimal outlays produce countless benefits for a business. What is especially good about resilience is that it does not cost much. Most elements of resilience are either free or inexpensive and mostly require determination. Actually, while we do buy certain elements of security, resilience cannot be bought but only built from what we already have. Encouraged communication, ownership, cross-functional collaboration, flexibility, and generally improved security culture will certainly bring along numerous collateral benefits to any commercial organization. This certainly makes it cost effective and worthwhile the effort.

SELF-ASSESSMENT/DISCUSSION QUESTIONS

1. How would you rate the flexibility of your organization to successfully address unanticipated harmful events?
2. Would you classify the security culture in your company as satisfactory?
3. Do you think that your organization learns lessons from security flaws and constantly improves?
4. Does your model of governance involve security clauses in standard operating procedures?
5. Do you have an annual security training matrix that lists the training requirements for all the employees in your company?

CHAPTER 11

Marketing and Security:
The Appeal of Target Hardening

INTRODUCTION

We usually regard marketing and security as two functions in an enterprise that are the furthest apart in the corporate space and without any real influence on each other. Although, in practice, there is almost no real communication between the two, the actual possibilities and opportunities that would arise from closer cooperation are enormous. Security is one of the basic human needs and an important particular that influences the perception and decision of consumers. While the need for security and, consequently, the importance of security in our everyday activities and decisions is growing, companies continuously fail to use the opportunity to attract consumers and tackle sales by using the value that their security adds to the product and the entire business. Actually, security plays an important role in all of the 4P of Marketing (Product, Promotion, Place, and Price). Security does not only protect the Product but also shapes it; as one of the primary human needs, the concept of security can assist in Promotion; Security protects the Place, whether physical or virtual where actual sales can happen and ensures that the product will be where and when it is needed; finally, as risk and price depend on each other, security or lack of security will influence the price of the product. Moreover, it can be exactly security that could be the prevailing factor in ruling out the competition.

> Although the importance of security in our everyday activities and decisions is growing, companies continuously fail to use their security to attract consumers.

The Overlap Between Marketing and Security Strategies

The correlation between security and marketing starts with seemingly prosaic issues, such as how the information that we post on the company website affects its security, or if car fleet branding will jeopardize the security of company's executives by exposing their affiliation. We certainly live in an era of

145

From Corporate Security to Commercial Force. DOI: http://dx.doi.org/10.1016/B978-0-12-805149-8.00011-X

oversharing, probably as we do not regard bits of information as pieces of a puzzle but more as separate concepts depending on which part of the company is dealing with them. Marketing and security constantly run into each other and overlap in their activities, sometimes successfully and sometimes with less success and with even harmful consequences. And still, in both cases the influence that they have on each other is purely accidental. Basically, many marketing actions will influence the security of the company while the security measures will influence its reputation and the image of its product. It is logical that the close coordination between marketing and security would help avoid the failures and achieve successes that would positively reflect on the bottom line.

Marketing and security often accidentally overlap in their activities.

Case Study: ATM Skimming

In 2012, a bank that I was working for has been trying out different, often expensive, technology solutions to tackle skimming. Skimming is a method that fraudsters use to obtain credit card information illegally. This is done using a small electronic device called a skimmer that is placed on an ATM and used to swipe and store hundreds of victims' credit card numbers. Some technology solutions were unsuccessful from the start but some managed to lower the number of skimming with limited success and only for a while. Instead of continuing the technology race that the bank was evidently losing to criminals, as the bank's Chief Security Officer (CSO), I decided to try another, much less technical approach to solving the skimming problem. Because the skimmers were gray like most ATMs, the criminals had close to unlimited choice as to where to install the devices in a way that they would not be visible to clients. Because my bank had a relatively small number of ATMs, I assumed that if we were to change something in the physical appearance of the ATMs, the criminals would be better off continuing to use the skimmers on other banks' ATMs that remained the same rather than adapting the skimmers to our bank ATMs and then being able to use them on only a small number of ATMs and losing the majority. I managed to convince the management of the bank and the marketing department to paint the ATMs red, which is the corporate color of the bank. Moreover, during negotiations with the vendor, the bank managed to get the manufacturer of ATMs to manufacture the ATMs and spare parts in the new color at no additional charge. In the security sense, the strategy worked, as it managed to stop the skimming incidents. Moreover, the change received overwhelming support, not only from the marketing department of the bank because it supported the visibility of the brand, but also from bank's clients as they could have now identified bank's ATMs more easily.

THE ROLE OF SECURITY IN CONSUMERS' DECISIONS

Marketing could be simply defined as a professional effort of satisfying the needs of consumers for products, service, and agendas better than the competition and in a profitable manner by using the 4P of Marketing. I also like to define Marketing as focused placement of stimulating information aimed at achieving a goal by engineering the emotions, behavior, and decisions of targeted groups. In order to influence the emotions and decisions, marketing professionals require proficiency with the primary needs of the groups that they want to reach. We can divide needs into two concepts: consumers' real needs and perceived needs. One of the most common models of marketing aimed at engineering the perception of need is Fear Marketing that is based on pointing out the (often false or exaggerated) consequences of not using a certain product or agenda. Fear Marketing is often used for political marketing, in health awareness campaigns, but also for advertising a wide variety of products. Probably the oldest and the most successful use of Fear Marketing is in advertising and spreading religious beliefs. Still we rarely use Fear Marketing when fear is legitimate and there actually could be real consequences for the consumer as a result of not using certain product or service. Basically, even when our product is safer, or can improve safety, we rarely use it in our marketing efforts to attract consumers and discredit the competition, apart from occasionally advertising our commitment to comply with environment, health, and safety standards in order to emphasize the quality of the product and our social responsibility. On the other hand, Fear Marketing sometimes simply emphasizes what the consumers already know. A good example of the use of Fear Marketing is the Greek Tourism marketing campaigns for the summer of 2016 which pointed out the security risks that accompany other otherwise attractive holiday destinations, especially North Africa and Turkey, and presented Greece as their secure alternative. Consequently, in 2016, Greece experienced an overwhelming increase of the number of tourists. Also, as Greece outraced the competition, lodging prices also drastically increased compared to previous years.

> Companies rarely use the legitimate fear of consumers to offer the solutions that they have.

Certainly, when we talk about perception, another task of marketing is to raise the perceived value (brand equity) of a product, for example through branding, or create the bargain perception of a product, for instance through Asymmetric Dominance (or Decoy) Marketing. The principle of Asymmetric Dominance is to raise the perception of value or create the perception of bargain about a certain product through comparison with another product whose only purpose is to serve as decoy. Basically, advertising a cell phone that we want to sell together with another cell phone that has the same or higher price but weaker features will direct the consumers to the better deal product. Still, can security be the point that will direct consumers to our product instead to the similar and similarly priced product offered by competition that does not have security as part of it? It certainly could be.

Also, we should not forget that, the more successful marketing becomes in engineering the perception of a certain product or agenda as a need, and raising its perceived value, the more important it is for a consumer to ensure its possession and protect it from harm.

Actual Risks and the Feeling of Being at Risk

Why are Zombie apocalypse preparation books bestsellers and why is there a growing demand for "Zombie proof" equipment and apocalypse survival kits? In order to analyze the actual marketing and sales potential of security, we must first try to reach the conclusion about the importance of security in our routine and especially the role that it plays in the decisions that we make. However, we have to go beyond analyzing only the existing or probable risks and their remedy. We can also divide security in two concepts, actual security and the feeling of being secure. Moreover, risk is also two different concepts: being at risk and feeling threatened. Basically, the perception of risk and the feeling of security do not necessarily always match actual risks and actual security. While our understanding of the real threats and actual security depends on our firsthand experience, the feeling of being at risks and the feeling of being secure depend mostly on the information that we are exposed to, whether they are funded or not.

> We can see the sales potential of security only when we analyze the importance of security in decisions that we make.

Still, during the process between creating a need and actual sales, there could be numerous influencers that will modify the perception of consumers about the product, add new needs, or simply physically prevent the product from being in the right place at the right time. With globalization, consumers' brand loyalty is naturally decreasing. With a big number of choices, consumers can easily and quickly replace one brand for another. Even a seemingly insignificant flaw can chase away consumers. Moreover, with globalization, it is not only products that travel faster but so do bad news. So, while Marketing did engineer the perception of need for a certain product or service, it is the job of security to assist sales by providing the conditions that will lower the probability that a consumer will reconsider, give up, or satisfy that need by buying from the competition.

The Motivation of Consumers

Many studies that analyze the motivation of consumers put security at the top of the list of human needs that are essential to all selling, whether face-to-face or in advertisements. Most marketing communications appeal to one or more of these desires:

- Security
- Possessions
- Imitate others
- Good health
- Sexual and romantic drives
- Curiosity
- Love of beauty
- Play and relaxation
- Feel important
- Physical pleasure and comfort
- Love of others
- Avoid discomfort

Moreover, while security is namely one of the needs, it is the essential ingredient of many of other listed desires. Security is basically the assurance of possession, health, comfort, and relaxation. It is emotions that sell, and fear and remedy against it are even more successful than sex or desire in triggering emotions. It goes without saying that we would be more keen to prepare for the approaching hurricane than for the upcoming Fashion Week.

> Security is not only one of the basic human needs, but also the essential ingredient of most other needs and desires.

PRACTICAL USE OF SECURITY IN MARKETING

Although, by now, the connection between marketing and security should be rather obvious, how can we practically use security in the actual marketing of products and services? It is true that the model in which security contributes to the product and the relevance of security for marketing a product varies. Actually, security is often more usable when explicitly advertised in marketing campaigns of services than those of physical products. In certain cases, such as in the hospitality industry, the relevance of security for the product and service and the marketing appeal of security are equal. Basically, security is namely one of the criteria that would (or should) determine if a guest would choose a certain hotel and as such it would be logical to use security as a factor in marketing campaigns. The same goes for, for example, airlines and airports, internet providers and cell phone operators, software manufacturers, companies that are handling the sensitive data of clients, etc.

In some cases, the way that security supports a product is much higher than its actual marketing potential, but not nonexistent. For instance, the important role that security plays in protecting the integrity and ensuring the safety of drugs in the pharmaceutical industry, or basically any manufactured product, is obvious. However, emphasizing security in the marketing campaign for medications would not actually make much sense as it would not really appear relevant to the consumer unless the aim of the communication is to address legitimate concerns.

On the other hand, in certain cases, the marketing value of security is higher than its practical importance for the specific product or service. Having security guards in bank branches is more about addressing the clients' need to feel secure than providing actual security. Basically, security officers are in many cases not trained or equipped to solve security issues, starting even with the minor ones, and are usually correctly instructed not to even try to resolve incidents. Bank clerks are for instance mostly instructed not to contradict perpetrators in case of a robbery and to actually comply with their requests in order to minimize the damage that could otherwise expand from purely material damage to injury or even loss of life. Furthermore, as the bank is most probably insured against financial loss, the actual professional role of security officers can be summed-up as service aimed at discouraging unprofessional wrongdoers. On the other hand, the more important role of security officers is marketing. So, although branch security officers have nothing to do with banks' efforts to protect their clients' sensitive information, funds or transactions, security officers basically serve as displayed manikins that should reassure the deeper concerns of clients and show that the bank has security taken care of on all levels.

> In certain cases, the marketing value of security is higher than its practical importance.

Does a Security Presentation Work?

The simple reason why security presentations are effective is the human fascination with concepts and labeling, the urge to simplify terms, and consequently the ability of our brain to fill in the blanks based on the information that we do have. For instance, by advertising a certain product, we try to direct the consumers to conceptualizing the entire lifestyle that comes with the product. For security marketing, we can take the example of the security guards in the bank. A client would, based on the visible security measures, without performing an actual vulnerability analysis, form an opinion if the security of the branch is simply good or simply bad. He/she would then use this opinion to build a much wider conceptual image of the overall security of the bank and label it as successful or not successful. This image will be an important particular in forming an opinion about the overall effectiveness of the bank. Naturally, the overall appearance of security officer will play a big part in forming that image.

Using the Growing Importance of Security

The importance of security in everyday life is changeable and is certainly changing. So, how do customers perceive security measures? While in the past businesses were mostly concerned with the level of tolerance of their customers to security measures which were necessary for the business, they should be now mostly concerned with the level of tolerance to the lack of security that is the result of cost saving. One good example of such a trend is the aviation industry. Once, airline companies and airports were concerned how their clients will accept the heightened security measures and if their profits will suffer from the situation that was actually forced upon them by terrorism. Less than 10 years later, security established itself as one of the most important criteria of travelers when choosing an airline and transit airports. We can look at this phenomenon as a successful two-step Fear Marketing campaign in which it was terrorism that pointed out the potential consequences and the aviation industry that offered the remedy with unbeatable arguments. Basically, security became so much part of the aviation folklore that it would be difficult to separate them, even in the unlikely case that the need for security would drastically decrease.

Missing Opportunities

A much less successful story is the example of the hospitality industry. While terrorist attacks against hotels are actually much more frequent than attacks against airlines, hotels still have a long way ahead to completely understand how to turn it around and benefit from it. So, although many hotels indeed drastically increased their security, they are keeping quiet about it and not using security in their marketing campaigns. Even without the recent epidemics of devastating terrorist attacks that should have been a cold shower for the hospitality industry, the bond between core services provided by hotels and security should be unbreakable. On the Maslow Pyramid of basic human needs, just like on every similar list that addresses human needs and human concerns, security is ranked as the second most important one, just after physiological needs such as to drink, eat, and breathe. On the other hand, hotels base their marketing campaigns on almost all the apparent and latent desires of guests but somehow manage to usually completely neglect security as a basic requirement and an important particular that influences the choices of guests, and consequently its role as a valuable marketing tool. The Cornell University study on hotel security, which was conducted in the USA, found that hotel guests in general have a high acceptance of most security measures along with the willingness to pay extra for some of them [1]. Unfortunately, not only that hotels do not use security to boost sales and increase profits but, as they still regard security as a combination of cost and hustle that will result in bad image and consequently loss, they try to hide it from the guests in order to minimize the damage.

> In general, many hotel guests are willing to pay extra for heightened security measures.

Advertising Security Improvements: Challenges and Opportunities

Why do we advertise improvements in the core performance of a product or service but are reluctant when it comes to advertising security improvements? For example, we will easily emphasize the new better formula or a more practical packaging in the marketing campaign for laundry detergent. On the other hand, we will completely bypass security in our marketing efforts, even following a major security issue that is directly related to our product. Absurdly, we believe that by advertising improvements of the core features of the product, we demonstrate our continuous efforts to satisfy the growing needs of consumers while, by advertising security improvements, we admit that we were actually not doing it that great in the past. Moreover, we believe that, by emphasizing enhanced security following a disaster, we are actually taking the responsibility for it. One of the core reasons for neglecting security is definitely also the widespread belief that mentioning of security reminds us of security risks and that it, as such, creates discomfort and deters potential customers. This, however, mostly refers to the physical aspect of security as the situation concerning Information and Communication Technology (ICT) security is quite a bit different, probably as we do perceive security as the core elements of new technologies. So, following a threat or a larger scale security breach, most ICT companies will race to inform about the newest security upgrades. However, although the risks of losing information, money, and privacy are certainly terrifying, they are still not the type of risks that involve the possibility of physical injury or loss of life. So, an important reason (or excuse) for not advertising physical security improvements is our instinctive understanding that traditional, physical risks are our primary concerns and that, as such, they are a sensitive subject with too much weight to it, even for advertising. Ironically, the more vital and basic a security issue is, the more we tend to neglect it in our campaigns. On the other hand, we are forgetting that we have both the responsibility and the opportunity to address the legitimate, basic concerns of consumers and that a bolder approach would certainly be rewarded.

> We often race to advertise improvements in the core performance of a product but are reluctant when it comes to advertising security improvements.

Case Study: Hotel Security Courses in Kenya

In the beginning of 2015, following a series of terrorist attacks in East Africa, I was asked to prepare and deliver a Security Seminar for Hotel Executives in Nairobi, Kenya in cooperation with a local hospitality management college. The main idea of that particular course is to strengthen the ability of hotels to combat crime, terrorism, and fraud by helping the decision makers to understand security and its practical application in the hotel industry in addressing specific risks. The course also substantially addresses the interconnectedness between service, privacy, and security and how visible target hardening can add to the positive experience of guests and deter potential wrongdoers. However, the list of requests that I have received from the client in the final stages of the preparation for the course contained a rigorous demand that I basically completely change the nature of the course and concentrate on teaching them how to mitigate the risks in a way that the guests will not notice (and be bothered by) security. Unfortunately, my client has completely failed in understanding and addressing the needs of hotels and their guests. First of all, as the Kenyan hotel industry did indeed suffer material losses due to canceled reservations which were the result of terrorist attacks in the country, minimizing the risk of attacks certainly called for tighter security measures. On the other hand, unless they are visible to guests, security measures will not address the quite different, but equally important factor which is the feeling of guests that they are at risks and making them feel secure. Sadly, this case is not only relevant for the Kenyan hospitality industry but is an example of how business globally continuously fails to address the needs of clients to feel safe and promote security that they actually have in order to tackle sales.

ROLE OF SECURITY IN RAISING THE PERCEPTION OF VALUE

Security is certainly not a product. However, security is often part of a product and can be a valuable part of sales efforts. Still, security companies advertise and sell security as a product while, on the other hand, commercial enterprises rarely use the actual role that security plays in their service and for their product. As security is a desirable situation that has to be reached through a process, security companies actually sell what they do not have to clients that actually need it. On the other hand, businesses often do not sell what they do have—the added value that security gives to their product. Actually, as more expensive products require more protection, it is logical that the importance of security in presenting the product to customers grows with value. Consumers look for qualities that confirm the price. If a product is expensive, they are going to look for signs that confirm that value. However, value is not a synonym for approachability. Actually, value is more related to exclusivity than to ease of access. Many brands raise the perceived value of their product by using various techniques to present it as unique, exclusive, and more difficult to acquire. For instance, a famous luxury sports car manufacturer adds additional prestige to its products by creating waiting lists and delaying the supply of its vehicles to customers.

Basically, in order for sales to happen, customers need to see a value in purchasing the product or service. For customers to actually perceive value, it has to be communicated through marketing, emphasized during the entire sales process including during distribution and on the actual point of sale, and finalized with the quality and experience that a consumer will receive from the product.

THE ACTUAL AND THE VISUAL QUALITY OF SECURITY

Unfortunately, we rarely see that the marketing potential of security is being completely utilized. However, by neglecting it, companies are not just missing opportunities but actually creating a negative image. So, as much as good security presentation could be effective in building a good image, a bad one will not only ruin the perception about the security of the company but also damage the reputation of the entire company. Companies are visually communicating with their partners, clients, and customers not only with the logo but basically, everything that they present (or do not present) makes a statement. A well maintained facility, exclusive location and, for example, good visible security measures also speak to customers. We should not forget that it is actually security that is a service which is put upfront and as such, will be one of the first elements that will influence the opinion of guests about the business. The lack of security or if it is obviously weak and only "pro-forma" (such as outdated systems and inadequate personnel and setup) will show that the company does not invest in some of the crucial processes. It would give an impression that the product might only be packed in a nice wrapper but that the fundaments are weak. Basically, if the company is saving on security, what else is it saving on? Also, the lack of security implies that it does not value its product and the overall business enough to protect it. Naturally, if the company does not value itself enough, it should not expect others to value it more. The message is even graver if that product is a service that requires safeguarding of the tangible and intangible property of clients, their wellbeing, and their confidential information (as in, for example, hotel and lodging industry, financial institutions, providers of ICT services, or law offices) where lack of security does not only imply that the company is not protecting its own assets but also their clients'.

Although we often believe that our clients are "security blind," and that they will pay attention only on how core services are presented and marketed, that is far from being true. Security is not only visible but actually very much eye-catching. So, as we have mentioned before, it is the security presentation that counts as much as the actual security, and sometimes unfortunately even more. So, as much as visually appealing security in bank branches can add to the visual quality and the overall image of the bank, a bad security presentation would be much more harmful than having no security at all and not attracting attention to it.

ADVERTISING AS A TARGET HARDENING TOOL

As much as security can assist in promoting the company and its products, marketing can play an important role in assisting security by using its channels to deter potential perpetrators and at the same time advertise the company and its product. If it is true that there is no bad PR, there is certainly no bad PR in publishing favorable information about a company, even if the information is not about its products but about its security. Basically, target hardening is the marketing of security as its role is to deter potential perpetrators by warning them about the quality of security. Apart from the actual security setup that serves as deterrence as much as it has a practical value, Target Hardening is also performed through different models of manipulative communication starting with simple warning signs and posters, but also by using media to publish information or disinformation that would mislead or discourage potential malefactors. A Target Hardening presentation is sometimes the mirror image of the real security abilities of the organization but is often also intentionally exaggerated. As we have mentioned earlier, while mostly perceived as identical, actual security and the feeling of security are in practice quite different although they certainly do influence each other. So, as much actual security will inspire the feeling of being secure, a security presentation will dishearten offenders and by that strengthen actual security. A company that would use the media for Target Hardening by associating itself or its brands with higher security will profit on several levels. First, and obviously, it would benefit by improving the tangible security of the company. Second, it would achieve higher exposure. Moreover, publishing favorable information that do not necessarily concern the brand would be refreshing for the consumers that often do get tired from the aggressive sales approach and product focus of companies. Third, by adding security to the image of the company and its brands, businesses positively influence the consumers' image of the company and the perceived value of its products by adding reliability, uniqueness, and luxury.

SECURITY AS A COMPETITIVE FACTOR

Using security to present a product as more valuable (and priced the same) than the one of the competition by advertising security is actually a useful tool that can be used as Asymmetric Dominance (Decoy) marketing. Although it is still a road less traveled, security is actually an important asset that can make the difference when competing with quite a similar, and similarly priced product or service. However, many businesses use the interconnectedness of value, price, and risk in a completely wrong way. So, instead of using security to increase the value, many businesses use the lack of security to decrease the price. Basically, many companies will opt to save on security so that they could decrease the prices instead of investing in security and using it to raise the value. Still, if we compete solely on price, the only result will be lower income.

> Instead of using security to increase the value, many businesses use the lack of security to decrease the price.

CHAPTER SUMMARY

This chapter analyzes why we are hesitant when it comes to using security in marketing. However, the truth is that the main reason for neglecting the marketing potential of security is not the result of an educated conscious decision based on a thorough marketing analysis but actually that it simply never crossed our mind. We basically often allow our narrow expertise to overshadow logic as we prefer to stick with the comfort zone of our occupation, instead of expanding competences by exploring wider opportunities. With security organizations often being marginalized in commercial enterprises, security professionals are rarely encouraged to voice an opinion that is not directly related to what is believed to be their competences. On the other hand, Marketing is often far from even considering security as a marketing tool. Certainly, without a real decision and a coordinated "top to bottom" organizational effort to use the benefits of cooperation, there could be no move to the right direction. Extracting the marketing value of security calls for understanding and using the importance that security has in our daily routine and the power that it has on our choices and decisions. We should constantly ask ourselves what are the security features that appall to consumers and how to use them. Moreover, we need to continuously analyze where are marketing strategies and our security strategies meet, and how this meeting point will improve both our security and our sales.

SELF-ASSESSMENT/DISCUSSION QUESTIONS

1. How would you rate the level of cooperation between marketing and security in your organization?
2. Does the growing importance that security has in our everyday lives relate to your product or service?
3. Do you pay attention to the visual quality oy your security and the effect that it has on your partners, clients, and consumers?
4. Could use security as competitive factor?
5. Are you aware of the role that security has in shaping your product or service and do you believe that that role is assumed and recognized by consumers?
6. Do you believe that good visible security adds to the feeling of uniqueness and luxury?
7. As brand loyalty is generally decreasing as outcome of globalization, do you believe that the reliability provided by security assists companies to retain customers?

Reference

[1] Cornell University School of Hotel Administration, Safeguarding Your Customers: The Guest's View of Hotel Security <http://scholarship.sha.cornell.edu/cgi/viewcontent.cgi?article=1052&context=articles>, 2006.

CHAPTER 12

Sales Potential of Security: Security as Ingredient of the Product

THE BOND BETWEEN SALES AND SECURITY

There is no doubt that for a business to exist, it needs sales. Sales equal revenue, and revenue means the business can operate. It is naturally the final step in the value chain and the reason why a business operates in the first place. Security is certainly vital in assisting sales in its mission to get the product to the consumer. However, when assessing the ways in which security supports sales, we usually do not think beyond its role in physically securing the Supply Chain, protecting the product in Retail, and safeguarding the integrity of the brand. We basically mostly get stuck in comprehending the physical support that security provides to sales without thinking about how the concepts of security can contribute to the concept of selling. We have already established that security contributes to all the 4P of Marketing. Naturally, sales uses the channels created by marketing to supply the product or service to the consumer.

The concepts of security can contribute to the concept of selling.

SUPPLY CHAIN

Most initiatives to manage security as a core business functions rotate around the role that it has in protecting the product in the supply chain. Logically, the supply chain is often the weakest security link in the route of getting the finished product to a consumer. We do everything to protect the product in the factory and in retail by creating and executing relatively long-lasting security strategies. However, in order to manage the security of the product in the supply chain, we require continuous involvement and recurring creativity. Unfortunately, as we have already mentioned, security in commercial organizations mostly focuses on responding to issues and controlling steady processes instead of continuously creating strategies and planning. Consequently, our supply chain often receives the same treatment like a static facility instead like a moving target. We usually end up sending a truckload of valuable

159

From Corporate Security to Commercial Force. DOI: http://dx.doi.org/10.1016/B978-0-12-805149-8.00012-1

products from the factory to retail protected with inflexible and uncreative security measures without taking into account the complexity of transport. Basically, we usually rely on inflexible technology instead on breaking the routine and coming up with safe route plans. Moreover, supply chain security is often understood as a synonym for technical systems used during the transport of goods. Distributors usually perform deliveries using uniformed and visibly marked vehicles with marketing slogans and pictures of products which make it easy for criminals to track them and follow them. Deliveries are mostly performed at the same time, in the same way, and according to the same route plans while relying only on technology to protect the products. We actually often forget that even the newest cutting edge security systems quickly get an antidote and become pretty much useless as independent measures.

> Although even cutting edge security systems quickly get an antidote, supply chain security is still regarded as a synonym for technology used during the transport of goods.

Security should certainly be the integral part of the supply chain, owing to the frequency, cost, and disruption potential that security incidents can have during transport of raw materials to production and during the transport of products from the production to clients and consumers. Security incidents during supply chain are actually very common and increasing in both frequency and severity, especially concerning the theft of hot products. Like any other business, goods are stolen to feed consumer demand; often the goods are ordered and even pre-sold before the theft. Based on the 2014 Global Cargo Theft Threat Assessment issued by FreightWatch International Supply Chain Intelligence [1], apart from metal, whose popularity is increasing, other, more traditional hot products are those that are easily disposed of and yet retain a high black market value. Such products include alcohol, computers, entertainment equipment, mobile phones and other small electronic devices, luxury clothing brands, cigarettes, and prescription drugs. Cargo theft is a growing threat occurring across the world. Easily resalable goods represent the largest share of stolen property, but criminals are willing to steal almost anything. Also on the rise are the number of assaults on drivers and the increasingly violent nature of supply chain incidents. Whereas various forms of theft are still the cause of most loss, armed hijacking has shown a significant increase in many countries. The most frequent road transportation security threats include the involvement of drivers, curtain slashing, moving vehicle attack, load diversion, impersonation of police officers, and forced stop [2].

> Supply chain security incidents are very common and are constantly increasing in both frequency and severity.

Primary Distribution

In primary distribution, huge amounts of goods are transported by trailers to distribution centers. It is preferably performed via highways and involves distribution centers mostly located on the outskirts of large cities, avoiding urban or remote areas as much as possible. Stealing the content of a trailer requires accurate planning, organization, and logistics. Basically, in order to steal that much merchandise and avoid being caught, the criminals need at least a transportation storage space of the same size, which has to be hidden, not to mention the ability to move goods to and from storage [2].

Secondary Distribution

Secondary Distribution is the transport of goods to clients. The main differences between primary and secondary distribution are the amounts of transported goods and routing. Secondary distribution is performed everywhere where there are points of sale for the particular product. Whereas the reward for criminals in primary distribution is much more tempting, it takes a lot of effort. On the other hand, secondary distribution is a much softer target and is equally attractive for organized crime and individual criminals. In secondary distribution, the worth of the contents of a van can be as much as €100,000 or more, depending on the goods, which is still a good motive. As we do not have the freedom to choose secure routes but have to use a limited number of choices in reaching the actual point of sale, the opportunity to execute a crime is often higher in secondary distribution than in primary distribution [2].

> The opportunity to execute a crime in secondary distribution is usually very high.

Maritime Supply Chain

Maritime supply chain security usually requires the involvement of security professionals specializing in maritime security. Risks can be divided into five areas: seizure of cargo, use of vessels for smuggling, use of vessels to launch an attack, sinking vessels to disrupt the supply chain infrastructure, and hijacking vessels for ransom. Regardless of contemporary threats that are constantly emerging against global importers, traditional models of cargo seizure, such as theft and maritime robbery (piracy), remain a severe challenge, especially for vessels carrying high-value goods and valuable liquids such as oil. The ability of the maritime supply chain infrastructure to move large quantities of goods provides an excellent opportunity for criminals to facilitate illegal drug trafficking, gunrunning, and people smuggling. After the 9/11 attacks, fears arose that terrorists might use a maritime supply chain to perform an attack, such as transporting a bomb by ship and detonating it in a port. However, the vessels themselves may be targets of terrorist attacks, as they have been in the past. Apart from the well-known hijackings for ransom in the waters of East Africa and other piracy hotspots, there are hijacking cases that are not financially motivated but actually support a specific political (terrorist) agenda [2].

RETAIL LOSS PREVENTION

According to the 2011 Global Retail Theft Barometer survey [3] generated by the Centre for Retail Researching in Nottingham, England, the total annual cost of retail theft exceeds $119 billion globally, amounting to 1.45% of total retail sales. The amount of money spent in 2010 on retail loss prevention totaled $28.3 billion worldwide. According to the same survey [3], employee theft accounted for 44.1% of retail shrinkage in North America, whereas external theft, including shoplifting and organized retail crime, was responsible for 43.2%. Products experiencing the highest percentage of thefts were clothing, fashion accessories, and high-value electronics and accessories, followed by health, beauty, and pharmaceutical products. The most common challenge that loss prevention faces as a discipline is balancing between preventing theft and shrinkage and providing good customer service. Aside from theft, the most significant retail crimes include burglaries, robberies, cash loss, bad checks, refund fraud, and exchanges of product at the counter (replacing the good item with a forged one). Still, the main reason for the loss of product is the simplest form of theft—shoplifting—which is mostly performed by amateur shoplifters and motivated by poverty. However, the number of thefts executed by career criminals is growing. Crimes such as theft and fraud committed by employees, or with the assistance of employees, are the biggest concern of retailers. Apart from stealing the actual product, internal theft includes the theft of cash and fraud against the store and against customers. Stealing merchandise and blaming it on external factors is the simplest and the most common form of employee theft [2].

The main reason for the loss of product in retail is simple shoplifting.

Security Presentation in Retail

In retail, security and a security presentation are equally important. Moreover, our security presentation in retail counts as much as any other element that we use in a store to attract customers. We deliberately chose the design, music, lighting, and personnel in our stores that add to the experience of customers and represent the product but often do not pay any attention to the appearance of security personnel that are usually the first people that a customer will see.

THE DISPLAY CABINET PHENOMENON

I have mentioned already that we usually deliver products to clients by using branded vehicles with marketing slogans. This marketing strategy increases our visibility but mostly completely contradicts our security strategies. Still, would it be possible to combine visibility and security and produce winning results for both security and marketing, and consequently sales? Although mostly not intentionally, and certainly not in a coordinated manner, marketing and sales professionals often actually use security to raise the perceived value of a product while security measures unintentionally raise its marketing appeal. I like to call this occurrence "The Display Cabinet Phenomenon." Basically, when evaluating the value of an item that is openly displayed and easily accessible on a point of sale, and the value of the same exact item that is locked in a display cabinet, consumers will typically assess the value of the protected item as being higher. The principle of display cabinet is also used as an aid in Asymmetric Dominance marketing. Basically displaying certain merchandise in a cabinet will give the consumers the feeling of bargain when compared to other merchandise that have the same price but are openly displayed. Although to marketing and sales professionals this occurrence is solely the result of the directed focus and added perception of value through presented luxury and uniqueness, I believe that luxury, uniqueness, and security are actually complementing concepts. First, the fact that an item is luxurious naturally classifies it as exclusive and less accessible. So, an item that is luxurious, and as such more valuable, needs to be protected. Second, the fact that an item is protected tells the consumers that there was actually practically less chance that it was damaged or tampered with before reaching them. While this example analyzes only the practical use of display cabinets in retail, the logic behind it is applicable to overall marketing efforts. For me, the Display Cabinet Phenomenon is a practical element of retail marketing and merchandising as it is a general concept that opens up the possibilities of using security to establish a positive image of the company and assist the branding of its products, services, and agendas by positioning them as unique and luxurious. Even politicians sometimes use visible security measures, such as bodyguards and escorts, in order to present themselves and their programs as more valuable even when they do not face any risks.

> Marketing and sales professionals often unintentionally use security to raise the perceived value of a product while security measures unintentionally raise its marketing appeal.

Case Study: Armed Robberies of Cigarettes in Secondary Distribution

In 2007, a premium brand cigarette manufacturer that I was working for experienced regular armed robberies during deliveries to points of sale. The robbers would wait for the van close to the point of sale, take the car keys at gunpoint, and drive away with the van. Within a short time, my team and I managed to design and implement a successful security strategy which resulted in the immediate end to robberies of the company's delivery vans. One of its key features, apart from breaking the routine of the delivery routes, was random security escorts that accompanied the vans to points of sale. The escorts were made noticeable by using marked security vehicles which were attended by uniformed security officers. However, they were performed without any logical order so that robbers would not be able to know what delivery van will be escorted and when, and would basically not be able to plan and execute robberies. Although this genuinely security strategy produced expected results as it successfully addressed the security issues, it also influenced the sales. While at first, my company had doubts if the presence of security will deter consumers, what happened was exactly the opposite. Unexpectedly, points of sale reported higher sales on days when the vans that were delivering them supplies were escorted by security, especially immediately following the actual deliveries. One reason was certainly the attention that the branded delivery vans and security escorts attracted together. Another reason was probably the perception of higher value that security added to the product. Basically, while the competitors sold equally good products with similar prices, by adding security to our brands we actually added exclusivity, luxury, value, and focus. So, although consumers mostly switched from one competing brand to our brand that had the same or similar quality and identical cost, they had a feeling that they are receiving more value for a bargain price.

THE CORRELATION BETWEEN RISK AND PRICE

Risks always exist, someone always needs to address them, and they always cost money. The question is if it will be us that will address risks or leave it to the client to deal with them. That is why price is almost always an indicator of risks. High price of a product shows that a company is trying to compensate for the risks that it is taking. On the other hand, low prices are a sign for consumers that they are taking a bigger risk when purchasing the product. Attractability does not equal lower prices. If we do nothing but compete on price, we are certainly selling ourselves short.

> Low prices are a sign for consumers that they are taking a bigger risk.

Security and Reliability

Apart from uniqueness and luxury, security is also a synonym for reliability. In general, for consumers, a higher price equals luxury which is the outcome of the combination of brand, performance, and reliability. So, while the quality of performance of the product is directly related to its purpose, reliability addresses the quality of its other features that are not necessarily visible, such as safety and security. Basically, as consumers, we expect all the elements of a product to follow the price. When we buy an expensive electrical appliance, we buy a brand, better performance, and more attractive design. However, we also naturally expect the product to be proportionally safer than its cheaper alternative. On the example of Fast Moving Consumer Goods (FMCG) or, for instance branded clothing, the higher the price, the more we believe that security is part of the reliability of the product and that, as such, there is less chance that it is not genuine or altered. By highlighting security, companies are actually adding value to the reliability of products and to the perception of quality. We actually outsource security daily. When we purchase a product or a service, we also purchase security and safety that go with it. So, for instance, instead of performing a thorough threat and vulnerability assessment every time before we purchase a product or a service, we outsource that concern by simply paying for it. However, when we emphasize security, we add additional value.

On the example of the Hospitality Industry, it is true that the guests might seem less interested in security measures, but only as the other services are put up front and are certainly easier to spot. However, less interested does not necessarily mean less concerned. The guests will mostly pay attention to the services that we are presenting, such as luxury, cleanness, service, and food and will assume that we have the infrastructure taken care of. So, as they would not inquire about the quality of power installations, thunder protection systems efficiency, and plumbing, they would assume that security is there and that its level is proportional to the quality of other visible services. So, what if hotels would actually tell the guests that they are saving on their security in order to be able to offer them cheaper rooms? It would not be any different from telling the guests that they are saving on the electrical infrastructure and other basic features, such as food safety, so that they could have an affordable holiday. However, it should be clear without even mentioning it that the quality of core services or products is assumed by consumers to be proportional to the quality of the infrastructure, including safety and security. While I do like to use examples from the hospitality industry, simply because of the most illustrative interconnectedness between service, privacy, and security, the principles definitely apply to all trades. Consumers of FMCG products would assume that the manufacturer is investing efforts and resources to protecting the product from being compromised as much as bank's clients are confident that the bank is protecting their funds and their data. And still, many businesses use the "It will not happen to me" security strategy without investing in security unless an incident actually occurs.

However, security is assumed by clients and consumers only when everything goes smoothly. This (sometimes) unfounded confidence is very fragile and once it is even remotely compromised it requires tremendous efforts to reassure. Benjamin Franklin noticed three centuries ago that "it takes many good deeds to build a reputation and only one to ruin it." Moreover, repairing a bad image (and bad security) will end up being incomparably more expensive than an initially efficient security organization would have been in the first place.

> The fact that clients might seem less interested in security doesn't necessarily mean that they are not concerned.

Security and Price

The relationship between business and customers is complex when it comes to valuing a product. Actually, customers are quite detailed in assessing the tradeoff between value and cost and determining if it is a fair one to make. We want consumers to buy our product and not be discouraged by prices that are too high or confused by prices that are too low. Finally, we want to profit from it. Putting a price tag on a product is one of the most challenging parts of the relationship between a business and a consumer. A customer will buy a product if he/she determines that the price is worth paying. Certainly, the ratio between price and the actual quality of the product is an important factor in consumers' decisions, but not the only one. The value that we offer to customers is the combination of quality, the convenience of buying it, the importance of having it, our marketing and sales efforts, the level of risk that a customer is willing to accept, and how pricing follows all the other elements. For instance, we might be willing to pay more for a product in the grocery store on the corner than spending valuable time to find a store where we could buy the same exact product for less. Also, we will often pay more if the higher price means that the risk of using the product is lower. We are actually accustomed to associating lower prices with risks. For example, we know that the prices of a product in a supermarket will drop as the expiry date is approaching.

> We will often pay more if the higher price means that the risk of using the product is lower.

We can take the example of the Tunisia hotel industry, following a wave of terror attacks in the country, to illustrate the relationship between risk and pricing. After the terror attacks in Tunisia in 2015, especially the mass shooting attack that occurred at the tourist resort at Port El Kantaoui during which 38 tourists were killed, Tunisia Hoteliers were faced with a dilemma if to decrease the prices of rooms in order to attract the guests that were scared off or leave them as they were. Most hotels decided to drop the prices and use it as decoy. However, naturally, this strategy did not produce expected results. It was actually clear to most of the potential guests that the prices have decreased because of the risks as price and risk are interdependent. Basically, the higher the risk, the lower the price. Furthermore, the gusts were not discouraged by the prices in the first place but by the risks. Also keeping the prices as they were and pretending that nothing has changed would not do much good either. So as absurdly as it may seem at first glance, a successful strategy would have to be based on advertising security improvements and even backing it up with higher prices. Basically, in case we are presented with a challenge (which terrorist attacks certainly are), every action or lack of action makes a statement. When offering cheaper service, we are stating that we are aware that the risks exist and that our guests will be compensated for accepting it. When keeping the prices as they were, we are mocking their genuine and well-founded concern by pretending that nothing is happening. With tighter security and higher prices, we are telling our clients that we are aware of their concerns and that we are actually doing something about it.

Expectations and Performance

Another important part of marketing and selling is matching the expectations of customers with the performance of the product. When translated to security, in case of risks, customers expect to see and experience security. However, in most cases, even when we do increase the level of security, we keep it hidden as we wrongly believe that visible security discourages customers. Unfortunately, not only that we hide something that people actually expect and hope for but we also aggravate the practical performance of security that they might actually need. First of all, we are taking away the target hardening effect that is intended to deter wrongdoers, which does play an important role in security. Second, regular security that invests efforts in being invisible will have less energy left to react. Also, security that is instructed to be concealed will naturally hesitate to react. Finally, by physically moving security away from where it should be, we slow its response.

By hiding security from customers, we fail to live up to their expectations.

One of the reasons for the extent of the tragic outcome of the terrorist attack in Nice, France, on July 14, 2016, when a terrorist drove a truck into crowds celebrating Bastille Day, killing 86 people and injuring 434, is certainly the assessment of the French authorities that the heavy presence of security forces would take away from the spirit of the celebration. The lack of sufficient numbers of police officers during the event unquestionably weakened their abilities to prevent the incident and slowed-down the response. France had previously, several months prior to this particular attack, experienced several devastating terrorist attacks. Basically, not only that such an event required enhanced security measures on the operational side, the participants to the celebration also mostly expected to see and experience security. During the celebration and following the tragic event, many witnesses publicly complained about security measures that they perceived as below expectations.

CHAPTER SUMMARY

Everything that a company does comes down to finalizing the product as intended, preserving it in the intended condition while getting it where and when it is needed, and being paid for it. If we actually put it that way, it becomes clear that security should not be support to sales but actually its integral part. Unfortunately, many companies barely have security setups. Even when they do have a security organization, these organizations are in many cases marginalized, often outsourced, and are mostly only dealing with simple manned guarding, let alone being able to provide any real support for the business and its core processes that extends beyond pure access control and patrolling. Although security certainly plays (or should play) an important role in physically protecting the product and its integrity in the supply chain and during actual sales, security is not only a service but also a concept and a feeling that can become a valuable addition to sales strategies. We should understand the way in which risks shape prices, remember and use the abilities of security to raise the reliability and the perceived value of a product or service, and benefit from the remedy that we provide.

SELF-ASSESSMENT/DISCUSSION QUESTIONS

1. How much attention do you pay to the appearance of security officers in places where they interact with customers?
2. Do you believe that a good security presentation could assist your sales efforts?
3. In case of your product or service, do you believe that you will achieve greater benefits by saving on security and offering lower prices or investing in security, advertising it, and charging more?
4. In case of risks, do you think that customers expect to see and experience security or that they will be only reminded of the risks and bothered by it?
5. In your organization, how well does security function liaise with the sales function, starting from analyzing concepts and planning joint strategies and up to the point of physically getting the product to consumers?

References

[1] 2013 Global Cargo Theft Threat Assessment, FreightWatch International Supply Chain Intelligence Center <www.freightwatchintl.com/node/1602>.

[2] M. Cabric, Corporate Security Management. Challenges, Risks, and Strategies, Butterworth-Heinemann, Oxford, 2015, pp. 151−165.

[3] The Centre for Retail Researching, The 2011 Global Retail Theft Barometer Survey, Nottingham, England <www.retailresearch.org/grtb_currentsurvey.php>, 2011.

SECTION V

Embrace

CHAPTER 13

Security Metrics: *Measuring Performance*

METRICS

Simply said, a metric is a system of measurement. Metrics tell us if our processes and strategies are giving results and if they are cost effective. They also direct us in improving performance and help us to understand trends. Moreover, they are a communication tool that connects security and business. In Information Security, we can find different, industry-based benchmarking groups where metrics are shared. Moreover, metrics are the integral part of information security, and there are countless available sources of measurement standards and best practices. On the other hand, in Physical Security, measuring is still a mystery. Security professionals are continuously struggling to come up with relevant metrics that would sum-up their performance, but also to find the way to escape from daily tasks in order to create the time to measure, plan, and assess. Many security professionals measure simply for the sake of collecting Key Performance Indicators (KPIs) so that they could communicate the results further and justify budgets. Of course, they still face the challenge of convincing their superiors that security metrics are import for the business. However, the biggest slipup is the common failure to understand that measuring is crucial for improving performance and that creating and using the system of metrics is not even close to being as time consuming as it may seem at first glance. Using metrics in all the processes, parts of processes and activities that together make-up the security organization of a company is certainly one of the key tasks of a Chief Security Officer (CSO).

> Security professionals continuously struggle to come up with relevant metrics that would sum-up their performance.

KEY PERFORMANCE INDICATORS

KPIs are the results of important metrics that we use to measure, monitor, and improve the success of a crucial activity that we perform. In addition to

173

From Corporate Security to Commercial Force. DOI: http://dx.doi.org/10.1016/B978-0-12-805149-8.00013-3

the role of KPIs for improving security processes, they are also a practice and a tool that can assist in bringing security and business closer to each other by justifying security strategies and explaining results while using the language of the business. KPIs are crucial for measuring the success of any function.

> Key Performance Indicators are a tool that can bring security and business closer to each other.

We know that each risk management activity should be detail in approach but simple in explanation. This principle is especially true when it comes to measuring KPIs that must be detailed when it comes to methodology, specific when it comes to the activity that we measure and our objectives, and simple when it comes to analyzing results and communicating them further. We actually often confuse measuring, simply for the sake of knowing with measuring our actual impact on an activity with the purpose of improving. We can measure anything but not everything is a KPI. Basically, in order to be classified as KPIs, metrics have to be understandable and relevant to the function that they are presented to and not only for the part of the business that collects them.

As they illustrate our performance, KPIs have to be the result of our actions and therefore influenceable. To be more specific, we can measure weather conditions. Still, this data cannot be influenced and most probably would not interest stakeholders. We can still collect data about the weather should we find it relevant, but we should not confuse collecting weather data with KPIs. Second, not even all measuring of performance can be called KPI. Out of numerous indicators of performance that we measure, only few of them have the potential to be regarded as crucial. For instance, we may measure the level of performance of our subordinates. This data would be important for us; it would be an indicator of our success and would influence our future approach in tackling performance. However, this data would be irrelevant for our superior who is only interested in the overall success of our unit and not in the separate performance of our subordinates. KPIs also must have the ability to be measured continuously as our key finding is the comparison between more results that were collected over a certain period of time. A one-time measurement is not a performance indicator. Naturally, continuous measuring requires a commitment. Also, KPIs must have logical timing. To be more specific, if we know that an incident occurs every few weeks, our measurement frequency should be set in a way that we can clearly understand trends and test the efficiency of the actions that we have implemented. For instance, if we would want to measure our success in a certain process where incidents usually occur once per week. For such a frequency of incidents, measuring and comparing results every week would be too soon to understand trends, whereas measuring them once a year would be too late to address issues efficiently and implement timely adjustments.

For metric to be precise, we must be accurate in the way that we collect relevant information, understand what influences it and be clear about the specific element that we want to measure and the specific process that we are measuring it in. We must also completely understand to what extent we can actually influence the result. If our objective is to reduce losses resulting from theft of goods during transport, our KPI should be loss, the department of concern is distribution, and we can, for example, base the measurement on the ratio between the value of transported goods and the loss over a measured period. By only recording the overall loss on the enterprise level, we will not be precise enough and consequently not able to use the findings to create strategies and measure performance. Also, by only counting lost products in distribution without basing it on the transported volume, we would misinterpret the results and our metrics would probably end up being misleading. Finally, one of the rules concerning metrics is that we should never use them to evaluate individuals.

> We have to know to what extent we can actually influence the results that we are measuring.

Example for the Loss KPI

To show the system of security metrics practically, we can take the example of a KPI for the loss of product (finished goods) during distribution. To have precise metrics, we have to define all particulars related to the measurement. For example:

- We are measuring loss
- The sector that we are measuring is Sales and Distribution
- The area that we are measuring is Metropolitan
- Our objectives are to follow the loss of finished goods owing to security incidents and test the effectiveness of steps taken to improve performance
- Our type of measurement is quantity
- The measurement frequency is quarterly

The explanation of the method of measurement is a comparison of the number of product units lost versus the previous measurement period. An index is created according to the number of product units distributed versus the number of product units lost. Data are to be collected according to accurate reports from the sales and distribution department. We will measure the number of products lost compared with the number of products distributed. Thus, the values we are measuring are:

- Total volume distributed
- Loss

X = total volume distributed (million items).
Y = loss (1000 items).

The loss index would be:

$$\text{Loss Index} = \frac{Y}{X} \times 100$$

If the amount of distributed goods over the measured period is 6 million, our X value will be 6. If the amount of stolen goods is 3000 our Y value will be 3. Our loss index for the measured period (for example, the first quarter) will be 50:

$$\frac{Y = 3}{X = 6} \times 100 = 50$$

If, for example, in the second quarter our loss index was 33.3 and in the third it was 16.6, this means that the KPI is showing a positive trend.

Example of Incident Measurement

When we measure incidents, we can be misguided if we measure only one dimension of incidents, such as their direct financial impact on our organization. For example, if we measure only loss, we will not know whether the loss occurred because of the small number of large-scale incidents or many minor incidents. However, this information is crucial if we are planning to design a successful strategy aimed at mitigating losses. Basically, we want to classify incidents that occurred over a certain period, based on two factors: severity and frequency. Moreover, we want to have a standardized approach to measuring that would allow us always to have the same standards when classifying incidents.

To have a standardized approach, we will simply classify the loss that occurred during an incident, for example

- Low loss—under €1000
- Moderate loss—between €1000 and €10,000
- High loss—between €10,000 and €50,000
- Extreme loss—over €50,000

We can classify the frequency of incidents by, for instance, creating a simple index based on the number of days a measured period has and the number of incidents that occurred during that period. If our measurement period has 30 days, we can decide that:

- Low frequency—up to five incidents
- Moderate frequency—between 6 and 15 incidents
- High frequency—between 16 and 30 incidents
- Extreme frequency—over 30 incidents

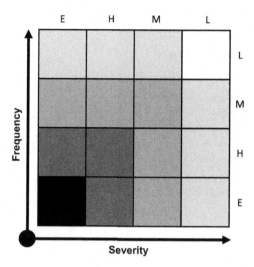

FIGURE 13.1
Incident measurement matrix.

In order to graphically present the two dimensions of incidents during a certain measurement period as a single result, we will typically use a simple matrix that combines severity and frequency. We can use a matrix shown in the example below (Fig. 13.1).

Measuring Severity

To add to the complexity of measuring, the severity of an incident is not determined only according to financial losses but also based on damages that are not directly financial and on the type of incident that occurred. For instance, if we only record direct financial losses, we will end up classifying an assault performed with a deadly weapon that resulted in severe injuries, but did not cause financial damages, as insignificant. Determining and measuring severity by taking into account the most impart particulars that form the blueprint of an incident will give us the real picture of the severity of an incident and bring us closer to understanding risks and designing strategies. We can use a matrix or a checklist to help us have a standardized approach when counting the severity of each incident. We can use the kind of matrix that is presented in the example below (Fig. 13.2).

Measuring the Consequences

Apart from only preventing losses and lowering the number of incidents, one of our important goals is to lower the impact of incidents. Therefore, we

A	Fatal consequences	600
B1	Major injury	500
B2	Moderate / minor injury	200
B3	No injury	0
C1	Armed assault	110
C2	Unarmed assault	100
C3	No assault	0
D1	Loss over 10,000 EUR	250
D2	Loss between 1000 and 10,000 EUR	100
D3	Loss under 1000 EUR	50
D4	No loss	0

A+B+C+D = Severity index

Low	< 50
Moderate	50 < 250
High	250 < 600
Extreme	> 600

FIGURE 13.2

Example of incident severity table.

cannot only measure the extent of loss per volume or the frequency of incidents but also the extent of loss per incident. Our objective is certainly to decrease the success (consequences) of an attack. A good indicator of our performance will be to know the average loss that we experience per incident and if that value is increasing or decreasing. Naturally, we must collect the data about all the incidents, including near misses and those that seemingly did not have consequences, and match it against the losses.

MISCONCEPTIONS ABOUT METRICS

Of course, extracting KPIs is not the only goal of measuring. We should measure the particulars that influence our performance even if some of the elements that we measure would not have the potential to be presented at the board meeting.

Almost all security functions in commercial organizations completely rely on the data received from measuring incidents and losses and regard it as the ultimate proof of performance. Actually, when we measure incidents we measure the combination of factors of which some we do influence and control and some we do not. Basically, by measuring incidents, we know how many incidents have occurred during the measured period. Still, we will not know with certainty if the lower or higher number of incidents was the result of our actions or not. The changes in the number of incidents could have been the result of less attempts due to numerous reasons such as decreased motivation of criminals or lower opportunity due to harsh weather conditions. Of course, we should continue to measure losses as they are the bottom line of security strategies and the point where security meets business. Still, if we completely rely on losses as the only measure of success, we have completely missed the point as we cannot rely only on the final outcome to understand if our strategies are successful, but also on the steps that we took along the way. Basically, if we measure only the outcome and not the process, in case of unsatisfactory results, we will not know which part of the process we need to improve.

> We cannot rely only on the final outcome to understand if our strategies
> are successful, but also on the steps that we took along the way.

Outcome Measurement and Process Measurement

In order to be able to have a balanced idea of our performance, we have to measure its two sides—the performance outcome and the performance drivers. Unfortunately, as we said earlier, most security professionals measure only the outcome without measuring the steps that they take along the way. Basically, in practice, security professionals spend most of their time responding to daily issues which does not give them enough time for strategic planning. Moreover, they are usually not able to allocate enough time to separately measure and assess their performance drivers, apart from collecting and presenting final outcomes of their strategies in the form of KPIs that are relevant for the functions that they report to.

Corporate security is a function that closely cooperates with the business management and all the functions that are concerned with security, safety, business continuity, and compliance to safeguard business interests, people, profits, and reputation and mitigate risks. It is responsible for guiding all employees into doing their part in the security system of an organization through their everyday actions and judgments. Logically, in order to really follow how they meet their objectives, security functions will have to be able to monitor and measure performance drivers, such as the amount and success of their communication.

Using Different Metrics in Different Industries

Logically, the way in which we collect and process metrics depends on our industry. For example, while in product-oriented enterprises, we can measure what we lose based on the volume that we produce or transport, in the industry of financial services, there is no relation between the volume and the performance of security. In most cases, we cannot put into proportion the effectiveness of our security measures based on our losses following a bank robbery but only according to the actual number of successful robberies, regardless of the extent of damage. Practically, once a robbery has started, security usually cannot control the amount of cash that will be stolen. Therefore, the extent of damage is not a performance indicator of the security function regardless of the fact that this is the particular that would mostly interest stakeholders. More so, the volume, which is in this case the amount of cash in the vault, has absolutely nothing to do with security metrics.

ACTUAL AND VISUAL QUALITY INDEX

We want to know if our physical security measures are effective both as a practical ability to protect and as a security presentation that is aimed at attracting consumers and discouraging potential wrongdoers. Naturally, measuring the actual and visual effectiveness of our security setup requires setting the standards that we want to measure which include all the particulars that influence both sides of performance. Firstly, as for our security presentation, we need to set the standards for the visual appearance of security people and technology that would produce the strongest effect. This is especially important if we are working with an external service provider and want to be able to improve the visual quality of our security which is an important aspect of its actual efficiency. Second, in order to measure the operational quality of our security system, we first have to know what we want from our security system to be able to articulate the desired outcome and turn it into standards. Finally, to measure the success of our security presentation and the actual effectiveness of our security system, we must create checklists to measure both the actual performance and the visual quality of our security setup that we would use during frequent unannounced inspections, checks, and drills.

MEASURING COMMUNICATION

As we have said earlier, one of the important missions of a security function in a commercial organization is interacting vertically and horizontally with all the people that are concerned with security and guiding all the people in an organization into doing their part in the security system. This element is an important step in reaching our security goals. However, in physical security, we often do not measure the success of this important objective.

In Information Security, measuring the success of our communication is quite a bit easier as it will usually produce immediate results in the behavior of employees which we can actually monitor. For example, we can know which employees read our emails, if they accessed the attached link, and how much time they spent exploring the particular page on the intranet. The concrete success of our awareness communication will be measured through the behavior of employees, such as their internet surfing habits or the number of cases, when unauthorized USB memory sticks were being used on company's computers.

In physical security, we cannot measure awareness unless an incident happens, or by performing unannounced drills and exercises which cannot be frequent enough to really assess our performance. On the other hand, we can, and should, measure the reach of our communication. Logically, the more successful we are in passing-on the message, whether upwards, downwards, or horizontally, the higher the probability that it will produce tangible results.

One way to communicate is certainly through annual trainings and refreshers that we deliver to employees. We can check the effectiveness of our trainings with tests that we will conduct immediately following the session and through occasional questionnaires that we will send out. Still, apart from trainings, we want to measure the reach of our day-to-day communication. Unfortunately, unlike in Information Security, the regular communication of physical security toward employees consists not only of electronic communication but also of hardcopy documents and posters as we want to reach also the employees that do not have a computer and an official email address. For instance, in a hotel, we are especially interested in building security awareness of employees that are likely to be the first to notice a problem, such as housekeeping staff, that typically do not use a computer as part of their duties.

Security is Marketing

In a way, security really is marketing. We are advertising and selling security to different target groups in the company. Logically, we want to know how successful our security marketing campaign was in terms of the number of people that it reached and the effects that it produced regardless of the media that we used for it. Some components, like posters, and other paper awareness materials, are hard to measure. In this case, we can virtualize the communication by placing QR codes on those materials. Basically, posters with the instruction to scan QR codes can give an indication as to how many people are paying attention to the communication, and even who are the people that accessed the communication from their cell phones and how much time they actually spent on exploring it.

> One of the key objectives of the security function is to advertise and sell security to different target groups in the company.

MEASURING THE IMPACT OF SECURITY ON CUSTOMERS

Most businesses are (and should be) concerned with how security will impact their customers and certainly want to determine if customers experience security as a feature that they benefit from or as unnecessary hustle. However, as measuring it seems like a significant challenge, many businesses would rather assume than measure. Basically, businesses prefer to accept security risks instead of risking customer dissatisfaction, without understanding that they might actually create dissatisfaction by removing security from customer service.

> Many businesses would rather assume than actually measure the level of satisfaction of customers with security measures.

We should first make a distinction between two sides of commercial security. Naturally, customers and clients do not benefit from all the security features of a company. The main purpose of commercial security is to protect the company, its assets, people, and profits. Still, some features of security also directly or indirectly benefit the customer, whether it is their actual security, security of their data, funds and assets, or the availability of the product or service when and where they want to purchase it or use it. When we talk about measuring the impact of security on a customer, logically, the more related security is to the customer, the easier it is to measure it. It is easiest to measure the satisfaction of customers with security in service-oriented enterprises where security is directly included in the service that they provide, such as hospitality and tourism, industry of financial services, providers of information and communication technology services, etc.

Of course, we will not know how our customers and clients perceive our security unless we ask them about it. Basically, basing our assessment only on self-initiated complaints and admirations of customers would be misleading. We also want to try to learn the standpoint of clients that did not volunteer their opinion. There is nothing wrong about telling customers and clients that we do take their security seriously, and asking their opinion about it, on the contrary. Naturally, by doing so, we will not only improve our customer service and reputation and deter potential wrongdoers, we will also be able to follow and measure how customers perceive our security.

To measure the impact that our security has on our customers, apart from collecting positive and negative reactions and queries we can create a system that is mainly aimed at measuring the impact of security on customer satisfaction. We can, for instance, use means of communication such as brochures and posters with QR codes that lead to the section on our website that contains a security excellence statement, a multiple-choice question, and the possibility to leave a comment. Naturally, if security is part of our service to the customers, the link to the security statement (commitment) page on our public website should also be visible to people that access the website directly. Of course, we should not base our metrics only on virtual communication but consider all the communication that we have with clients, such as queries at the front desk, book of complaints, and phone calls. We will classify the opinions of customers into five categories: Strongly Support, Support, Accept, Oppose, and Strongly Oppose.

Strongly Support

The group that can be classified as "Strongly Support" should consist of customers that support security by proactively expressing safety concerns, demanding a certain level of security, and even those that have complained about the insufficient level of security. For instance, in a hotel, guests that ask about hotel's security certificates at the front desk, leave favorable comments on the website, or are interested in purchasing additional security features, would be considered as strongly supportive.

Support

Customers that accessed the security statement page on our website and either chose the "support" option in the questionnaire or simply spent a certain amount of time exploring the page could be classified as supportive.

Accept

Customers that, for example, entirely complied with security measures without voicing their opinion will be considered as accepting. Basically, we can consider the lack of reaction of customers to security measures as accepting and favorable.

Oppose

Our customers that are in some way opposed to security will be classified as opposing. We will classify as opposed the customers that chose the "oppose" option on our online questionnaire or those that moderately complain about the level of security being too high but continue to use our services and products.

Strongly Oppose

We will naturally classify the deliberate disagreement of customers with our security measures as "Strongly Oppose". Basically, customers that have gone an "extra mile" to demonstrate their disagreement with the level of security by leaving comments online or in the book of complaints, writing protest letters and complaining verbally, will naturally be regarded as strongly opposing.

Results

We should mark the results using a bar graph and follow each of the categories separately. We should especially pay attention to supporting and opposing reactions to security and follow how their ratio changes. We will pay most attention to how certain events, such as terrorist attacks and published data breaches, especially those that relate to our industry, influence the opinion of customers. Naturally, we should exclude from these results the reaction of customers that are not related to the security setup but to the, for instance, individual performance of a security guard. Basically, not all complaints about security are opposed to security. We should use such complaints to improve individual performance of personnel but not regard it as proof of customer satisfaction or dissatisfaction with our overall security system.

MEASURING CUSTOMER SATISFACTION IN PRODUCT-ORIENTED ENTERPRISES

In product-oriented enterprises where customers have less contact with our security and in which customers will usually not be able to establish a clear, direct connection between security and the service or product that they are interested in acquiring and/or using, their satisfaction with security can be measured through its support to sales, such as availability of products on points of sales. We could attempt to measure it if we know how unavailability and downtime statistically impact customer loyalty and pay special attention to the flaws that were the result of security issues.

CHAPTER SUMMARY

Emphasizing achievements at all costs is a commonly used strategy in the internal corporate warfare (office cubicle combat) where we fight ambitions of others that contradict our own, struggle to gain managerial favoritism, and basically continuously try to find ways to survive in a competitive commercial environment. We all know the famous proverb that tells us that we do not have to run faster than the bear to stay alive, we just have to run faster than the guy next to us. The reality is that in corporate enterprises, a substantial amount of time and effort is wasted on running faster than others (selling ourselves and discrediting others) instead of escaping from the bear (solving actual problems). Consequently, measuring processes is often reduced to only collecting KPIs. Moreover, KPIs have become a marketing tool instead of being a utility aimed at measuring and increasing performance. Actually, we will rarely measure processes and activities, even crucial ones, if their results are not likely to be positive and if they are not attractive enough to be presented further and grant us a competitive advantage over others. However, measuring processes and activities for the purpose of following trends and improving performance is certainly one of the most efficient ways of reaching goals and accomplishing sustainable achievements. We know that in theory, measuring performance should be one of the key tasks of a CSO. Still, we often get confused when having to practically decide what a CSO should actually measure. Assuming that the job description of a CSO is well thought of and SMART as it should be, and that it contains all the performance drivers (What's and How's) and desired outcomes (Why's) that are expected from the function, it can also be regarded as a list of key processes and activities that must be measured, followed, and improved. Naturally, measuring performance must also be one of the key expectations from a security function and emphasized in its job description.

SELF-ASSESSMENT/DISCUSSION QUESTIONS

1. Does the assumption that security contradicts consumer service influence the actual and visual setup and performance of security in your company?
2. Have you ever attempted to understand how customers and clients perceive security and actually measure their level of satisfaction with it?
3. Is security part of your service or product and is it directly related to the experience of customers?
4. Apart from only extracting KPIs, is the security function in your enterprise encouraged to continuously measure and assess its performance drivers?
5. Apart from assessing performance, do you measure the visual quality of your security presentation?
6. Effective communication is one of the most important tools of security. Do you measure the reach and effectiveness of your internal communication?
7. Does the Marketing Department in your company assist security by improving the appeal of internal communication?

CHAPTER 14

Security Inventions:
Security Technologies in Business Analytics

THE TRANSFORMATION OF SECURITY TECHNOLOGY TO BUSINESS UTILITY

Companies sometimes buy more technology than they actually need. Especially in security, by not investing enough though, time and effort in choosing solutions that would satisfy both regulatory requirements and operational needs, we often end up having several technical systems that practically produce the same result. On top of that, we often acquire new technical systems that we want to use for various business purposes, without checking first if we already own solutions that can do that job. Unfortunately, security organizations are usually not the parts of the company where we will naturally look for solutions that could advance core business processes. However, many namely security systems that we use only for security can be extremely valuable for other business tasks, such as Business Analytics, Cost Controls, and Customer Relationship Management (CRM). Moreover, numerous systems that we consider to be traditional utilities when used for security would be innovative and advanced when used for core business, like measuring, analyzing, advertising, selling, and even improving the experience of customers in retail.

> Technical systems that are consider to be traditional when used for security are actually innovative and advanced when used in core business processes.

We all know the importance of the protective role of security technology for businesses. However, technological inventions that were primarily designed and used as security aids are becoming unavoidable business tools. For example, the use of access control software for the purpose of administration, such as controlling time and attendance, has become an essential part of Human Resources (HR) analysis and management while it is almost impossible to stumble upon a company whose supply chain does not use the Global Positioning System (GPS) technology to analyze and optimize delivery routes and lower fuel consumption. In recent years Internet Protocol Closed Circuit Television (IP CCTV) and Radio Frequency Identification (RFID) technology are taking retail chains by storm. Large retail organizations are

187

From Corporate Security to Commercial Force. DOI: http://dx.doi.org/10.1016/B978-0-12-805149-8.00023-6

switching from barcodes to RFID in order to simplify and speed-up processes but also because of the numerous other advantages of RFID for targeted marketing, sales, and business analysis. Moreover, with the invention of IP CCTV and the development of its analytical software, video surveillance turned into a complex system with the ability to analyze the behavior, movement patterns, and shopping habits of consumers.

Misuse of Surveillance Technologies

Unfortunately, when we talk about the use of security technology for analyzing and improving efficiency, the first thing that usually comes to mind is surveillance of employees. Basically, instead of using security technology to simplify and improve business processes, many companies misuse technology to increase performance by surveilling employees. Despite ethical, moral, and legal constraints concerning the unrestrained surveillance of workers, some companies prefer to sacrifices workers' rights for privacy and even risk lawsuits if they believe that it will increase efficiency and profits. The ways to monitor employees and their activities start with video and audio surveillance, network and call records, browser history and email retention, and unrestricted inspections of electronic correspondence. However, some companies even go an "extra mile" by using special surveillance apps on business phones to track the movement of employees and even thermal sensors to monitor their attendance.

One of the most frequently used models of surveilling employees is certainly through limitless inspections of their email correspondence. Basically, companies see it as completely legitimate to have unrestricted access to their own assets such as networks and systems. However, ownership does not justify breach of privacy. For example, while a restroom is also company's asset, it would be unethical to surveil it while it is occupied. We would not do it without a solid reason and relevant approvals, and certainly not without informing the employee about it.

Apart from being unethical and usually illegal, it is also disputable if increased surveillance is a better driver of productivity than increased motivation. Naturally, the two concepts completely contradict each other. Certainly, the use of security technology to surveil employees is greatly responsible for the lack of confidence of employees in the security function of the company and their support to it which affects its reputation and consequently its efficiency.

> It is arguable if increased surveillance of employees boosts productivity more than increased motivation that relies on the positive working environment.

ACCESS CONTROL

Access control is actually any system that can control entrance including a standard mechanical lock or a security officer at the entrance. Still, when we talk about Access Control Systems, it refers to a computer-based system that consists of special hardware and software. Apart from its primary role to control entrance to and exit from protected areas, access control evolved to a system with numerous other security and safety features, but also multiple functions aimed at simplifying the employee related administration, simplifying logistic processes, controlling the access to resources and their use, and saving costs.

There are several common types of Access Control cards (key cards) such as the mechanical hole card, barcode, magnetic stripe, smart cards embedded with a read—write microchip, RFID proximity card, and Wiegand wire embedded cards:

- Mechanical key card lock is a mechanical type of lock operated by a plastic key card with a pattern of holes which is equipped by sensors that detect the pattern.
- Barcode access control cards feature a unique barcode which will, when scanned by the reader, allow access to the restricted area.
- Magnetic stripe key card locks function by running the magnetic stripe over a sensor that reads the contents of the stripe.
- Microchip cards are embedded with a microprocessor that, together with a reader, creates electric contact which enables it to receive and send data.
- Wiegand wire embedded cards contain a small piece of specially processed wire that contains data which is read by passing it through, or bringing it near, a sensor.
- RFID technology in cards also contains electronically stored information. It uses electromagnetic field that allows the holder to gain access. RFID cards do not require a direct contact with a reader to be active but can even communicate with a scanner that is located far away.

Biometric systems rely on metrics related to human characteristics with the most common systems being the ones that identify users based on fingerprint, palm print and hand geometry, iris recognition, face recognition, and voice detection.

The third most common type of access control systems is keyless electronic locks that feature a keyboard and are encrypted with a code.

The main purpose of any access control system is certainly to monitor and control passage and access to areas and recourses while distinguishing between different predefined privileges set for different users or groups. Access control systems are constantly evolving with numerous options added to their primary role, thus expanding their use to areas that are not necessarily security related. Still, the security features of Access Control have remained more or less the same. Basically, the key security feature of access control technology is still to simply allow access to a restricted area to those that are permitted to enter and denying access to those that are not, while keeping logs. Moreover, regardless of how sophisticated they might be, solely technological solutions can rarely independently provide a sufficient level of security without being a part of the overall security setup. Basically, the change in a way that we lock and unlock a door cannot replace all the other crucial elements of security. We still need people to operate and maintain the system, and respond to issues, physical elements such as actual doors and walls, and procedures that regulate our security setup.

> While Access Control systems are constantly evolving, it is the features that are not necessarily related to security that are advancing, while their primary security role mostly remained unchanged.

Convenience

Despite their security value, electronic access control systems gained popularity also because of their convenience. For example, in the hotel industry, key cards almost entirely replaced traditional keys, not because of their security importance but due to numerous business reasons. Actually, security did not significantly improve with the switch from regular keys to electronic cards. On the other hand, electronic keys are cheap to produce, maintain, and replace as they only require an inexpensive plastic card with a magnetic stripe or Wiegand wire whose encoding can be completed in few seconds.

Traditional brass keys in hotels were purposely made bulky and heavy in order not to be convenient for hotel guests to take them along when they exit the hotel. One reason was certainly to prevent the keys from being lost and lowering the possibility of having the cost of replacing both the key and the lock in case of a lost or stolen key. Another reason was the ability to relatively accurately know which rooms are currently occupied or empty, based on the keys that are present or missing at the reception desk. This information would have been crucial for conducting an efficient evacuation of the hotel. By switching to key cards, hotels managed to drastically improve their key management practices, have accurate real-time attendance control, avoid unnecessary cost, and at the same time improve the convenience for the guests and their experience.

There are certainly numerous reasons for using Access Control systems instead of traditional keys. Instead of giving each of their employees a heavy key holder that contains keys to all the doors where he/she would be permitted to enter, they can simply issue them electronic ID cards with personalized access rights. Naturally, apart from only lowering security related costs and improving convenience, access control systems enable ease of access and higher work speed without sacrificing control.

Safety

Because of the ability to monitor the movements of people in real time, access control systems have a lot to offer when it comes to safety. Unfortunately, in practice, the safety advantages are usually not fully utilized. They are probably the most neglected features of access control. For instance, access control systems can be extremely useful in case of emergency, especially during evacuation and search and rescue as they offer the possibility to extract attendance logs and know who are the people that evacuate and who are those that failed to evacuate and approximately where in the building they could be trapped. In order to completely utilize this possibility, we require access control card readers on evacuation assembly points, the ability to quickly download attendance logs, and basic procedures that regulate the use of key cards during evacuation. Still, although access control systems can be the game changer during emergencies and are at the same time simple to use and not costly, they are only rare cases of companies that actually use them for those purposes.

> The important role that Access Control systems can play during evacuation is probably their most neglected feature.

Time and Attendance

In addition to its security features, access control systems are widely used to simplify employee related administration and increase the efficiency of their employees by controlling time and attendance. Many companies also conveniently use key cards to, for instance, verify the identity of employees in the canteen and manage their monthly canteen budget, or for controlling the use of company's vehicles in conjunction with GPS technology.

Cost Control

Apart from the lower cost of key production and maintenance, the most obvious example of cost saving using access control systems is in the hotel industry where electronic key cards are being used to control the power consumption in guest rooms. However, there are also numerous other ways to control costs by using key cards as identity verification utility. For instance, some manufacturing companies use key cards to control access to tools in order to prevent employee theft and embezzlement while some retail organizations attempt to prevent employee fraud by using electronic cards to verify the identity of cashiers that are using the register. Also, companies increasingly use key cards to limit the usage of office supplies, by connecting card readers to company's printers and photocopy machines in order to control spending.

Electronic Key Cards Versus Other Access Control Systems

Key cards are certainly the most popular technology used for physical access control because of its simplicity, low cost, high accuracy, and social acceptability. Basically, even the security risks associated with a card being stolen can be minimized with additional measures. For instance, card readers can be connected to monitors that will show images of employees that are using the key cards. Visual verification of identity is mostly used at the entrance to protected facilities and is monitored by security officers. Moreover, all card holders are required to immediately report a missing key card so that it could be deactivated and replaced. Many companies also intentionally keep their access control cards unidentifiable, by not adding any names or company logos that could associate the accidentally lost card with a facility where it can be used.

> Electronic key cards are the most popular physical access control solution because of simplicity, low cost, high accuracy, and social acceptability.

Access Control systems that feature a keyboard and are encrypted with a code are not as nearly user friendly or secure as access control cards. Typing the code certainly takes longer than simply placing a card on the reader, it requires that the user remembers the code, and in cases that more than one person uses the particular lock, it is impossible to know which one actually entered the protected area. In order to be simple to use, codes have to be short, which makes them vulnerable. Shoulder surfing (obtaining confidential data by looking over the victim's shoulder) is the simplest way of stealing codes. Also, codes can even be hacked by examining the dirt marks on the keys and guessing the pattern.

Biometric access control systems, such as facial, voice, fingerprint, and iris recognition, are much more difficult to break than keyboard codes. However, such systems are not always accurate. For example, a person's voice can change because of the mood or due to a simple cold, while background noises can make the system practically unusable. Different haircut, facial expressions, glasses, makeup, or facial hair can influence face recognition while fingerprint or hand geometry recognition could be affected by the position of the hand or finger, dryness of skin, or dirt on them. Biometric systems are often also expensive, they require a lot of memory for data to be stored, and they are often too slow to be efficient and are not always accepted as they sometimes raise privacy or health concerns. When it comes to their use in emergency, such as during evacuation, they are usually more of an obstacle than a benefit.

GLOBAL POSITIONING SYSTEMS

The GPS is a satellite-based navigation system that was developed in the period between the late 1970s and the mid-1990s by the U.S. Department of Defence. It soon gained popularity in the civilian sector, especially in private security, as a useful security tool, because of its ability to pinpoint locations and track movements. Although it was originally designed as a military locating and tracking utility that was eventually enhanced by adding various additional security and safety features, GPS technology has evolved into being irreplaceable in our daily routine. In addition to using GPS technologies as security tools and tracking utilities, companies widely use them to simplify cargo related administration, for car fleet optimization, and as a cost saving utensil.

Security

Apart from positioning and tracking movements in real time, GPS systems work as remote transmitters and receivers that offer numerous additional security features, such as remotely locking and unlocking vehicle doors and blocking engines. The system is also able to alert in case of a breach of predefined protocols, such as an attempt to open the vehicle door or cargo outside of the permitted zone. GPS devices are often equipped with a panic button that can be used in case of emergency, whether in a vehicle or as a personal handheld security device. When connected to a video surveillance system, GPS can, in case of an incident, turn on the hidden cameras in the vehicle that will record and save, or livestream the footage. Apart from being used in vehicles, aircrafts, and vessels, GPS technology is also being used to monitor the movements of people, animals, and objects.

GPS as Cost Saving and Efficiency Utility

Organizations are continuously looking for new ways to reduce costs and optimize processes. GPS technology proved to be extremely useful when it comes to car fleet management, especially because of the role that it can play in controlling and saving cost and work efficiency. GPS can monitor the behavior of drivers such as routing, speeding, uptime, and downtime that influence both efficiency and costs. For instance, by detecting and controlling speeding and other driving behaviors that directly lead to higher fuel consumption, we can also lower fuel related costs. GPS can also be used to make delivery plans and find the most optimal routes. We can also, in real time, locate and direct drivers to avoid traffic crowding or find the closest vehicle in case we have to pick up sudden deliveries. Another way of saving cost is through smart maintenance by determining the right time to pull vehicles off the road for maintenance based on actual use and identify issues before they actually happen.

> Apart from its security convenience, GPS is an important part of almost every efficient car fleet management because of its role in controlling and saving costs.

Limitations of GPS

Global Positioning Systems (GPS) are generally useless in indoor conditions as radio waves will be blocked by physical barriers, such as walls, and other objects. Also, regular GPS cannot pinpoint locations to greater than 3-m accuracy. Due to those limitations, GPS cannot be used to, for instance, track the movement patterns of retail customers in a store and analyze their shopping habits. Since few years, new technological solutions that are capable of accurate indoor positioning are emerging. Those technologies are specifically intended to be used for tracking customers in large retail organizations, especially for the purpose of targeted personalized advertising. Basically, such systems help personalize the messages that shoppers receive while walking through a store.

INTERNET PROTOCOL CLOSED CIRCUIT TELEVISION

IP CCTV is a type of digital video surveillance system that can send and receive data via a computer network and the Internet. Its ultimate benefits are flexibility and adaptability, enhanced performance, and easier installation. The invention of IP CCTV as opposed to traditional analog CCTV was an enormous step that has not only drastically improved the security features of surveillance but has transformed video monitoring from an exclusive security technology to an invaluable business tool.

> Internet Protocol Close Circuit Television that started out as an advanced form of security video surveillance has become as invaluable business tool.

Quality and Convenience

Firstly, IP CCTV typically uses high definition video cameras that greatly outperform traditional analog cameras in every segment that concerns image quality. This enables IP CCTV software to actually perform tasks that require outmost clarity, such as automated biometric recognition and video analytics. IP CCTV also makes sending and receiving data between sites easy which is especially useful for multiple site businesses such as retail chains. Moreover, video content can conveniently be delivered to mobile devices and laptops where different users can have different levels of access and action privileges.

Video Analytics

Essentially, video analytics is the ability of software to analyze video data and extract specific information that the user is looking for, based on predefined criteria. The primary goal of video analytics software was to increase the efficiency of security surveillance by minimizing the risk of human oversight and reducing work overload. For example, IP CCTV software is able to recognize items, such as weapons, that a security guard might have missed when watching the feed. However, video analytics software comes with a wide range of features that not only improve security but can also perform a variety of business tasks.

Use of IP CCTV for Retail Analysis and Customer Relationship Management

Not only that IP CCTV considerably improves retail loss prevention, it also significantly improves actual sales. Basically, parallel to protecting products in a store from a security point of view retailers can also track which products and designs attract most visitors to the store by using software to analyze traffic, walking patterns, and time spent in front of certain displays. For instance, by using heatmap analytics, retailers can determine the hot zones around the store where customer activity is the highest. This information can help stores to improve traffic flow, and make changes in the way the merchandise is arranged and displayed, so that it will be more appealing for customers and will encourage them to spend more. Additionally, video analytics can go as far as identifying what shopping habits apply to specific categories of customers based on gender, age, or preferences. For example, IP CCTV video analytics software can distinguish between different movement patterns of male and female customers, but also divided according to age groups. Also, software tools can follow customers that bought a certain product to understand what other products they are usually interested in. This information can help retailers in arranging and grouping products based on customers' preferences or understanding where they should advertise certain articles in order to produce the best effect.

> Video analytics can go as far as identifying what shopping habits apply to specific categories of customers based on gender, age, and preferences.

IP CCTV systems can also significantly improve one of the main causes of customer dissatisfaction—retail check-out queues. Software can alert the staff when queues exceed predefined thresholds in order to open additional cash registers. This will not only improve efficiency but, more importantly, improve the experience of customers and consequently their retention levels.

Issues Regarding IP CCTV

Apart from higher price of equipment, the only downside of IP CCTV as compared with analog CCTV is that keeping and streaming high definition video content requires significant amounts of internet speed and storage space.

USE OF RFID TECHNOLOGY IN RETAIL

RFID technology uses electromagnetic fields to automatically identify and track tags that contain electronically stored information. Technologies that use radio waves have actually been around for quite some time. Devices that rely on radio waves were first used in 1940s for military espionage and to distinguish between allied and enemy aircrafts. Modern RFID technology that is the closest to what we use today first appeared in 1970s and was originally used for automatic tolling and vessel identification, electronic credit cards, and for personal security identification, access control, and surveillance.

When we think of Radio Frequency in retail, we usually think of Electronic Article Surveillance (EAS) which is a technological method of loss prevention. EAS is based on Radio Frequency tags that are attached to items that will be detected by a scanner at the exit if a product containing the active tag is removed from the store. However, RF tags and RFID tags are not the same although both work using Radio Frequency.

As opposed to RF EAS that is a security tool, the main purpose of RFID is to be used for commercial data collection and as identity verification utility. RFID is typically a small electronic device that consists of a chip that can contain up to 2000 bytes of data and an antenna that enables the device to communicate with the reader. While a plastic card with a magnetic stripe can also store data that is used with a scanner, the advantages of RFID are that multiple tags can be scanned at once and from a distance, without positioning the tags relative to the scanner.

Use of RFID in Retail Versus Barcodes

While both RFID and Barcode technology are product tracking and data collection systems that can be used in the supply chain, the way in which they work is completely different. When it comes to the speed and overall efficiency of scanning goods, Barcode is no match for RFID. Basically, with RFID, approximately 40 RFID tags can be read at the same time and from a distance of up to 100 m. Moreover, RFID tags can contain valuable data such as product maintenance information and expiry dates. For example, retail employees can, within seconds, know what is on the shelves, what is missing, and what requires attention or should be replaced. RFID technology also offers numerous other possibilities. For instance, apart from only tracking and identifying goods, RFID can be used as a valuable tool in CRM and personalized advertising. On the other hand, Barcodes are much smaller than RFID tags and therefore easier to use. While RFID tags consist of computerized chips that have to be assembled and inserted into the product which makes it costlier, Barcodes can be printed onto practically any material which is a tiny overall cost as it basically only requires printing ink. Still, as opposed to Barcodes, RFID tags can as such be used multiple times.

Use of RFID Technology in Customer Loyalty Cards

Already for some time, many retail organizations have been using electronic key cards to verify the identity of customers at the counter by embedding chips or magnetic stripes into plastic loyalty cards. However, recently, some retail companies have started using RFID technology in order to be able to detect customers from the moment they enter the store, or even when they are just walking past the store. This allows the retailers to target customers by sending targeted promotional messages and notifications to their mobile phones. Unlike with loyalty mobile phone apps, customers do not have to perform any actions to be detected by the retailer, other than carrying loyalty cards in their pockets or purses

> Radio Frequency Identification Technology allows retailers to target customers by customizing promotional messages.

Using RFID Technology to Improve the Experience of Customers

A relatively novel use of RFID technology is in combination with readers that are embedded into shopping carts that can detect all the groceries or purchases that have an RFID tag. Such scanners are able to query all of the RFID devices that are in the tray, display its content on the monitor, and immediately total the overall cost. Additionally, smart shopping carts that combine RFID technology and specially developed software could, based on the content of the cart, suggest other matching products and inform the customer about current discounts. When used in conjunction with customer loyalty cards, smart shopping cart systems can completely personalize the shopping experience of customers by, for instance, displaying shopping lists and directing customers to listed items. Moreover, because of their ability to total purchases, smart shopping carts can also simplify cash register operations and lower the time that a customer spends waiting in a line at the cashier which is certainly an important part of the retail service. We can explain the cashier efficiency of RFID technology on the example of Electronic Toll Collection (ETC) which is greatly responsible for minimizing, and even eliminating delays that traditionally accompanied manual tool collection booths.

Saving Costs Using RFID

While RFID technology is definitely more expensive than its traditional barcode alternative, it does offer many more possibilities other than simply providing product information. The most obvious benefits of RFID compared to other product tags are certainly operational efficiency and cost saving. Basically, it takes a significantly less man-hours and consequently less staff, to complete operational and administrative tasks using RFID technology.

Common Problems with RFID

One common problem associated with RFID technology is the overlap of radio waves. Basically, as an RFID tag is unable to respond to parallel reader requests, the system must be carefully set to avoid collision and enable the tags to take turns when communicating with the reader. Another concern is accidental or intentional interference. Radio Frequencies used by RFID, which is similar to that of cell phones or Wi-Fi, can be jammed and disabled using the right electromagnetic frequency. Finally, one of the biggest dilemmas when it comes to using RFID tags in retail is finding an efficient way of removing them from a product once a purchase has been made, and reusing them in the supply chain.

CHAPTER SUMMARY

As we all well know, most businesses do not nearly invest in security as much as they should or could. Basically, as long as we measure investments only through quantifiable return on investment, we will naturally invest as little as possible in security, and often even less than that. However, although we might not be able to precisely quantify the actual security benefits of investing in company's security, we can measure the benefits that investing in security has on core business processes. The fact that we can protect our assets and at the same time receive measurable data that helps sell more products should be a good enough reason to re-evaluate our security technology investment criteria. However, regardless of how sophisticated our technology might be, the value we will receive from it will still depend on people. Technology will end up being useless without the vision and imagination of decision makers that invest in it, and without the skills and motivation of the people that operate it.

SELF-ASSESSMENT/DISCUSSION QUESTIONS

1. Is low cost of fair performance usually your main criteria when investing in security?
2. How much time and effort do you actually invest in assessing additional uses of technical solutions that you have, or are thinking of purchasing?
3. Do you believe that you are completely utilizing the business potential of security technologies?
4. In you company, is the decision on investing in security technology reached through a joint assessment of benefits (not only cost saving) by the security function and business functions?
5. Which business processes in your organization could additionally benefit from the technical solutions that were mentioned in this chapter?

CHAPTER 15

Practical Summary: A Systematic Guide to Managing the Security Function

CHANGE YOUR PERCEPTION OF SECURITY!

Not only that crime and terror have been flourishing in recent years but the shrinkage of distance as a result of globalization and due to the increased use of contemporary information and communication technologies to commit crimes and inform about crimes has brought security risks closer to ordinary people. As security threats started affecting all the spheres of life, people again became consciously aware that security and safety are their basic needs. Interestingly, while the need to be secure and the desire to feel secure are essential ingredients of almost all the decisions that people make, whether they are strategic or impulsive, routine or occasional, businesses still prefer to hide the actual security that they supply with their product or service from the consumers. One of the reasons is certainly that we are often so lost in designing innovative marketing strategies that target hidden desires that we forget about targeting the most important human needs. As for security threats, the biggest security risks are not crime or terrorism but the lack of understanding by decision makers (see Chapter 1: Commercial Security Challenges: *A Historical Perspective* and Chapter 10: Resilience—*The Wider Concept of Security*):

- Remember that security is one of our basic needs that influences, and should influence our decisions and actions, whether personal or business, routine or strategic.

The dilemma if security is mostly an expense for a company with little or no strategic influence on the actual business, or if it actually adds value to it should have been resolved a long time ago. We still may argue if security is indeed a key business process or valuable support to business processes. However, it should be clear that security is one of the crucial elements of a business that shapes the culture of the organization, its processes, products, reputation, reliability, customer service and client confidence, and finally profits. Moreover, security is not only a department but primarily an overall concept that requires the active involvement of all and will eventually benefit everyone

201

From Corporate Security to Commercial Force. DOI: http://dx.doi.org/10.1016/B978-0-12-805149-8.00028-5

(see Chapter 1: Commercial Security Challenges: *A Historical Perspective* and Chapter 3: About Corporate Security: *The Function, its Philosophies, and Practices*):

- Security in a commercial enterprise is not only a function but a concept that is managed by the security function.
- Security in not a quick-win project but an ongoing process.
- Every concept starts from the top. While it is the security leadership of an organization that leads the security of a company from a professional side, it is the business leadership that shapes it by initiating, hiring, arranging, giving authority, endorsing, supporting, and funding.
- Developing security competences is an important journey for business professionals. Security Acumen should be positioned high on the list of essential business leadership skills in every commercial organization.
- Security is a culture. There can be no security unless all the people in the organization understand their personal significance for the concept, know their specific role, and actually do their part in the security system.

ASSESS AND ANALYZE!

In general, by arranging security according to stiff standards and not according to identified needs, we will logically end up having parts of the business where our security measures exceed the needs and are as such not cost efficient, other parts of the business where measures are insufficient, and only a limited number of optimally protected business units. The logic behind making assessment-based security decisions is equally applicable regardless if we are talking about designing the security arrangement for a chain of local retail stores, or designing the security setup and strategies for international business units that make up the global operations of a company. Naturally, considering local specifics when making strategic decisions is not only important for security but for also compliance. Imposing the same standards from the center of power to all business units saves time and ensures that the entire company is following the same strategies and obeying the same rules. However, centralized model of governance usually does not take into consideration specific local risks and local regulations. Basically, companies, especially those that engage in international financial services, are required to comply with various local security standards in each market where they operate, that were determined by local regulators. By blindly applying one security model to all circumstances and markets, we do not only risk incompliance with local regulations but will also end up spending more once we finally purchase compliant solutions that are typically similar to what we already have (see Chapter 6: Quantifying Information Security: *Calculating the Intangible*; Chapter 8: Costs Saving and

Cost Avoidance: *Security as the Usual Suspect*; Chapter 9: Security Outsourcing: *A Double-Edged Sword*; and Chapter 14: Security Inventions: *Security Technology in Business Analytics*):

- Security assessments help you tailor strategies to specific circumstances and actual risks, and save costs.

MAKE AN EDUCATED DECISION ON WHETHER TO OUTSOURCE OR NOT!

We can say that outsourcing has become a trend. Companies increasingly outsource support functions, especially security, often without precisely weighing potential advantages and possible disadvantages. Actually, many businesses outsource their security organizations without examining if outsourcing would actually be successful, cheaper, easier to manage, or even functional, when combined with their industry, specific business model, local circumstances, and products or services (see Chapter 8: Costs Saving and Cost Avoidance: *Security as the Usual Suspect* and Chapter 9: Security Outsourcing: *A Double-Edged Sword*):

- The decision whether to outsource your security organization or not should be based upon a thorough analysis and assessment, and not be a result of blindly following trends. An outsourced security organization is not suitable for every business model and not necessarily more effective, easier to manage or cheaper.
- To keep the security organization in-house or to outsource it must be the joint decision between the business leadership (cash) and the security leadership (skill) of the organization.
- Remember that you are only outsourcing operators and not their performance. Whether you are outsourcing or not, remember that you cannot buy security. It will always be your responsibility to design, create, shape, manage, and maintain the security of your company.

HIRE SMART!

Hiring security professionals is also an assessment-based process. To hire smart basically means spending a bit more time on hiring specialists other than simply copying job descriptions and candidate requirements, and actually hiring according to concrete needs. It is unfortunately surprisingly common that recruiting processes for specialist functions in companies are performed without any involvement of professionals that actually know something about the specifics of the position. It starts from identifying needs, setting the requirements, advertising jobs, shortlisting professionals, checking credentials, interviewing, and all the way to the handshake (see Chapter 1: Commercial Security Challenges: *A Historical Perspective*; Chapter 3: About Corporate Security: *The Function, its Philosophies, and Practices*; and Chapter 7: Influencing Performance: *Running an Efficient Security Organization*):

- When hiring, make sure that you have someone onboard that can correctly assess your security needs, determine the requirements, and evaluate candidates.

SECURITY IS ABOUT BONDING, NOT ABOUT JAMES-BONDING

While both Information Security and Physical Security together contribute to the Security of the organization and should closely cooperate on that mission, the knowledge, experiences, and abilities required for these two functions, as well as mindsets, philosophies, and tools needed to perform and manage processes, are very different. Unfortunately, in order to save costs, companies increasingly combine Physical Security and Information Security by expecting one professional to wear two different hats. We can explain just how paradoxical that is if we look at this trend through the prism of exaggerated stereotypes. Basically, we chose between an ex-military person and a computer geek, expecting that either of them will be equally efficient in both roles. To converge does not mean saving costs by employing one professional that will manage all the aspects of security. It is better to have two specialist functions that successfully cooperate with each other than having one function that attempts to multitask. When we talk about convergence, we refer to the idea of managing both Physical Security and Information Security under one roof in order to address risks more efficiently by approaching them from different sides. Still, it would be fair to say that getting a person with a "field mindset" to efficiently align strategies and cooperate with his/her "virtual mindset" college, and vice versa, might not always be an easy task. However, making that relationship work would certainly be rewarding (see Chapter 1: Commercial Security Challenges: *A Historical Perspective*; Chapter 3: About Corporate Security: *The Function, its Philosophies, and Practices*; Chapter 6: Quantifying Information Security: *Calculating the Intangible*; Chapter 7: Influencing Performance: *Running an Efficient Security Organization*; and Chapter 10: Resilience—*The Wider Concept of Security*):

- You typically need separate physical security and ICT security functions that are working together and not one function that is managing both concepts. Both functions have an important role in protecting assets but mastering each expertise requires a lifetime of specialized learning, experiencing, and doing.

Probably the biggest misunderstanding when it comes to hiring and utilizing the expertise of security professionals is the linguistic confusion between Information Security and Traditional Security. Now that Information Security has completely adopted (or even hijacked) the traditional security vocabulary, it is in many cases impossible to determine if job postings are intended for ICT security professionals or for their physical counterparts. It is quite common that job postings for ICT security roles contain expressions like "Guerilla," "Special Forces," "Combat," "Soldier," "Hostile Environment Security Operative," "SWAT," and even "Border Control." Recruiters and ICT professionals are actually racing to find innovative combat-like (or game-like) names and decryptions for Information security roles which only contribute to the overall confusion that already exists (see Chapter 3: About Corporate Security: *The Function, its Philosophies, and Practices* and Chapter 6: Quantifying Information Security: *Calculating the Intangible*):

- Know what you need and what you need it for!
- Do not look for the competences that you want but for those that you need. Search for candidates with skills that you will actually use!
- Make sure that you are able to assess the candidates!
- Make it clear to both yourself and the candidates who you are looking for!

ALLOW SECURITY MANAGERS TO ACTUALLY MANAGE SECURITY!

To some, the fact that the security function should only manage security may come as surprise. However, Security is not a general utility that should perform tasks that no one else wants to do, including security, but a specialist function with clear agendas, goals, and much needed tangible support to business. Almost everyone that has ever performed security, in one way or another, in a commercial organization, has experienced being assigned completely unrelated tasks, simply because they do not relate to other specialist functions that their superiors are more familiar with or consider them to be more important (see Chapter 3: About Corporate Security: *The Function, its Philosophies, and Practices* and Chapter 6: Quantifying Information Security: *Calculating the Intangible*).

According to how it is perceived by laymen, security falls in the same category like sports coaching or politics—everyone thinks that it is easy, that they know how to do it, and believe that they could do it better. Business leaders should be familiar with security so that they could completely understand the role that security plays for the business: support it, and emphasize it, and not so that they could micromanage the security function (see Chapter 3: About Corporate Security: *The Function, its Philosophies, and Practices* and Chapter 6: Quantifying Information Security: *Calculating the Intangible*):

- Remember that security is a specialist function!
- When business leaders make security decisions, they often end up being pure business decisions that sometimes contradict basic security principles. You do not hire a professional so that you can tell him/her what to do. Diversity gives us different angles, opposed opinions, new ideas, and a coordinated multidimensional and multilayered approach to solving problems.
- In practice, the biggest portion of Security Manager's work consists of responding to daily issues that could typically be efficiently resolved by his/her subordinates. You will achieve the best cost and benefit ratio by encouraging security managers to utilize their expertise and concentrate on actual assessments, analyses, strategies, management, and measuring.
- Security must be linked to business goals while preserving its uniqueness and expertise. Protect its exclusivity by not turning it into a general utility.
- Micromanage the concept, not the function!

POSITION SECURITY HIGH IN THE HIERARCHY OF THE ORGANIZATION!

One of the important preconditions for security to be able to really influence top decisions and be directed by them is the place in the hierarchy of the organization that allows it to have a clear overview of all the processes in the organization, productively collaborate with the top management, present objectives, defend and show results, and align strategies. Typically, to preserve the objectivity of security, minimize the possibility of conflicts of interest, and increase its efficiency, the Chief Security Officer should report directly to the highest function in the organization—typically the CEO (see Chapter 3: About Corporate Security: *The Function, its Philosophies, and Practices*; Chapter 5: Quantifying Incidents: *Rethinking Loss*; Chapter 6: Quantifying Information Security: *Calculating the Intangible*; Chapter 7: Influencing Performance: *Running an Efficient Security Organization*;

Chapter 8: Costs Saving and Cost Avoidance: *Security as the Usual Suspect*; and Chapter 9: Security Outsourcing: *A Double-Edged Sword*):

- While it must be linked to business goals, the security function should also preserve its objectivity and independent professional judgment. Keep security protected from any internal politics and power struggles!
- The Chief Security Officer should report directly to company's CEO.

SECURITY FUNCTIONS SHOULD HAVE SEPARATE BUDGETS

An important issue that is closely related to the position of security in the organization is the budget. The usual problem related to security budgets, apart from amounts, is how they are approved and allocated. There are only rare organizations where there is a separate security budget so that security can actually receive the resources that it needs without risking that the money will be used for other purposes. In practice, security is usually granted just a fraction of what it originally asked for while it will usually receive only a fraction of what was approved. As much of it will typically be used by the higher function for sudden unrelated quick-win projects with higher exposure (see Chapter 6: Quantifying Information Security: *Calculating the Intangible* and Chapter 7: Influencing Performance: *Running an Efficient Security Organization*):

- Budgets are important for performance. Apart from the amounts, it is vital how budgets are approved and allocated and who controls them.
- In order to be efficient, the security function requires a separate budget.

COST EFFICIENCY IS A MINDSET, NOT THE GOAL

The global orientation toward cost saving, short returns of investment, and quick profits changed the once strategic nature of security by transforming it into a quick-win project. Almost all the corporate security projects are required to result in cost saving or cost avoidance, must have a short return of investment, and should produce almost instant results. Driven by corporate survival instincts, the primary concern of many security professionals in commercial enterprises evolved from security to finances. Basically, in many enterprises, security functions lost their uniqueness and identity and became general functions that mostly focus on cost saving (see Chapter 1: Commercial Security Challenges: *A Historical Perspective*; Chapter 2: Security and Economics: *From Global Causes to Local Circumstances*; Chapter 3: About Corporate Security: *The Function, its Philosophies, and Practices*; Chapter 7: Influencing Performance: *Running an Efficient Security Organization*;

Chapter 8: Costs Saving and Cost Avoidance: *Security as the Usual Suspect;* and Chapter 9: Security Outsourcing: *A Double-Edged Sword*):

- Security cannot be based around Quick-Win projects. It is an ongoing process that requires continuity.
- The security function should certainly be required to achieve goals in a cost-effective manner. However, its primary goal is not to save security costs at the expense of its operational ability but to have the optimal operational ability that will allow it to efficiently prevent costs and losses.
- Appreciate and protect the uniqueness and identity of security!

SECURITY NEEDS INCREASE WITH OPTIMIZATION

It would be fair to say that cost saving increases security and business continuity risks. The reduction of resources to the operational minimum with the tendency to extract the maximum from remaining resources did manage to cut operational costs. However, as a result, the resilience of organizations drastically dropped. Companies are becoming increasingly less flexible in preventing risks and responding to incidents, stopping their effect from spreading, and ensuring business continuity and recovery following a disaster (see Chapter 1: Commercial Security Challenges: *A Historical Perspective*):

- Security should not be regarded as fertile ground for saving. Although it cannot compensate for reduced operational capabilities, security should still be able to assist the business in ensuring continuity once operational resilience is reduced through optimization.

RETHINK RISK!

Risk Management is certainly one of the most important processes for a business. However, we often regard Risk Management as a function and not as a concept. Moreover, we artificially and wrongly divide risks into categories, the most erroneous of them being the classification according to financial and non-financial risks, thus neglecting the financial dimension of security risks and dismissing them for being less influential. Basically, instead of managing Risk by approaching it from different sides as a complex phenomenon, we split it into parts and approach each part separately with a single point of view (see Chapter 4: Risk: *Stuck Between Security and Economics* and Chapter 10: Resilience—*The Wider Concept of Security*):

- Risk is not just another term for bad investment.
- Every risk management activity should start with understanding the bigger picture of the causes of risks.

- Security risks typically accompany all core business processes and are the elements of all other risks.
- Apart from functions that are specifically tasked to manage risks, every corporate function performs risky activities and has risk management responsibilities.
- In order to efficiently address risk, we have to take into account an entire battery of factors that accompany each other and approach risk as a phenomenon with many dimensions and not as sporadic, isolated manifestations.

CHANGE YOUR UNDERSTANDING OF LOSS!

Quite similar to our, often shallow, perception of risk, we usually also have a very narrow understanding of loss. We often conceptualize loss as the direct outcome of an incident. However, an incident in one part of a process impacts the following stages of that process. Naturally, loss does not stop when an incident ends but actually only starts with an incident. The failure to really understand the reach and influence of security incidents and count their cumulated impact undoubtedly weakens the resilience of the organization (see Chapter 5: Quantifying Incidents: *Rethinking Loss*):

- Loss is the final outcome of a domino effect that starts with an incident.
- Make sure that you are able to understand and follow the real impact of a security incident on your organization and that you can quantify the overall accumulated loss!

LINK SECURITY TO THE TOP OF THE VALUE CHAIN

As the main role of security is to protect value, it should naturally be able to efficiently interact with the top of the value chain of the organization. Absurdly, in most cases, security is completely detached from parts of the company that are most responsible for generating profits, such as Sales and Marketing. When we think about the support that Security provides to Sales, we do not think far beyond the role of Security in physically protecting the product in the Supply Chain and in Retail. Moreover, we usually see no logical connection whatsoever between Security and Marketing. Actually, Security and Marketing have a lot in common. We could even go as far as to say that marketing is one of the most important tools of security. Basically, we deter criminals and terrorist by advertising security; we get support and funding by "selling" security to stakeholders in our organization; we use marketing principles and tools to get all the employees in our company to actively participate in our security efforts. Also, vice versa, the concept of security can be extremely valuable for the concept of selling and advertising. As one of the basic human needs, and consequently, on the basic requirements of consumers, security has an enormous, usually unutilized marketing appeal (Chapter 11: Marketing and Security: *The Appeal of Target Hardening* and Chapter 12: Sales Potential of Security: *Security as Ingredient of the Product*):

- Encourage the communication between Security and Marketing and Sales.
- Effective interdepartmental communication is essential for building resilience, generating new business ideas, effectively identifying and addressing risks, and aligning strategies.
- Think about how the concept of security can help you build and maintain your reputation, contribute to the attractiveness of your product or service, and consequently, how it can improve sales.

SECURITY IS NOT ALWAYS QUANTIFIABLE

We want to reach the situation when the ratio between threats and measures, as well as that of reasonable costs of measures and the cost of probable flaws, would be favorable for the company. However, we should quantify processes and base our decision on the results, only if we are certain that we can accurately determine the monetary value of that process. Putting a precise price tag on a process that is based on incomplete data and wrong calculations could end up being more harmful than basing decisions on simple intuition. The actual importance of security can be understood as protection from the consequences of multiple probable worst case scenarios that can happen in an organization. However, with the multidimensional support that security provides to the business, that is not only limited to loss prevention, but includes facilitation of all business processes, protection of reputation, and much more, it would be more accurate to determine the value of security according to its logical importance rather than attempting to calculate its numerical value (see Chapter 5: Quantifying Incidents: *Rethinking Loss*; Chapter 6: Quantifying Information Security: *Calculating the Intangible*; and Chapter 13: Security Metrics: *Measuring Performance*):

- Invest in security based on the importance that it has for your organization and the level of support that you want to receive from it!
- Basing decisions on the ratio between the cost of measures and the cost of probable flaws will usually be misleading.
- Security may not be quantifiable but its efficiency will still be proportional to how much we invest in it.

SECURITY SHOULD BE CAREFULLY BLENDED

Security system is a combination of factors applied to a variety of security principles that jointly aim at achieving protection goals. Both Physical and Information Security rely on the careful combination of all the following factors: People, Technology, Physical Protection Elements, Gathered Information, Effective Communication, Governance, and Leadership. While we need all the elements to have a security system, the proportion should depend only on risk assessments and vulnerability analyses (see Chapter 1: Commercial Security Challenges: *A Historical Perspective;*Chapter 3: About Corporate Security: *The Function, its Philosophies, and Practices*; and Chapter 7: Influencing Performance: *Running an Efficient Security Organization*).

Further, security is divided into three main periods: Prevention, Action, and Recovery. Each of the protection periods relies on some of the protection principles that are together referred to as 5D1R (Deter, Detect, Deny, Delay, Defend, and Recover). Prevention relies on deterrence, early detection, and the ability to prevent the problem from entering our facility or system (denial). Our response to an ongoing incident (Action) attempts to delay the problem from advancing and successfully defend what we are protecting. Finally, once the action part of the incident is over, we focus on preventing the domino effect of the incident from continuing to cause damage, minimize the harm, and return to routine (Recover). Naturally, the combination of all the seven factors of security should play a part in each of the 5D1R principles (see Chapter 1: Commercial Security Challenges: *A Historical Perspective*; Chapter 3: About Corporate Security: *The Function, its Philosophies, and Practices*; and Chapter 7: Influencing Performance: *Running an Efficient Security Organization*):

- Security is a precise blend of elements where the proportions depend on careful assessments and analyses.
- Favoring some elements over others and ruling out parts of the security system, only to change the nature of expenses or save costs has nothing to do with effective security.

BUILD RESILIENCE!

The security organization is only one part of the overall security resilience of a company, and consequently a part of its overall operational resilience. We say that risk is the effect of uncertainty on objectives. Resilience on the other hand is the ability of an organization to successfully address the effect of unfavorable events whether they were anticipated or not. Routine resilience is based on continuous efforts to understand risks and how they change and evolve and recognizing that every person plays a part in the efforts of an organization to detect and overcome challenges. However, the most important value of resilience lays in its ability to successfully resolve sudden, unanticipated, harmful events. Most organizations do plan the steps that they will take in case of unexpected malicious events and the security function is usually the one that designs and manages strategies. However, the most important precondition for effective resilience is well established channels of communication between all the people in an enterprise (Chapter 10: Resilience—*The Wider Concept of Security*):

- Resilience is the umbrella that unites all the functions around a common goal to ensure that the organization survives, meets its business goals, and prospers.
- There is no resilience unless security is considered a vital part of the business and all the people in the organization, horizontally and vertically, work together on reaching security objectives.
- Encourage effective communication between all the people in the company, both vertically and horizontally, even between functions whose cooperation may not seem vital for achieving business goals!

MEASURE!

Key Performance Indicators (KPIs) are concise and concentrated results of measures are relevant for the business and have been translated to the language of business. However, extracting presentable KPIs is not the only goal of measuring. KPIs are only the top of the measurement pyramid. Naturally, the most important mission of security metrics is not to determine if security strategies are cost effective but to understand if they produce desired results in the long run. Still, only collecting the final results of strategies will be quite useless unless we also measure the success of the steps that we take along the way (Chapter 13: Security Metrics: *Measuring Performance*):

- KPIs bring security and business closer to each other.
- Security KPIs are practical tools that drive performance and not marketing tools that should be used for personal promotion.
- We should not only measure the results of strategies but also the performance drivers that contribute to the success of strategies.
- Effective communication is one of the most important principles of any joint activity, security included. Measure the success of communication!
- Understanding how customers perceive our security is important. Do not assume—measure!

COMBINE RESOURCES!

We split complex companies into more manageable smaller specialized companies that we further divide into departments and units. Moreover, we create separate controllable budgets and follow spending through separate cost centers. We basically segment so that we can control. We even encourage competition in order to stimulate performance. However, we often forget that all the separate parts of the business should contribute to the overall goal of the company and that they can do it only if they effectively communicate, cooperate, and share resources (Chapter 14: Security Inventions: *Security Technology in Business Analytics*):

- Communication creates ideas, cooperation produces results, while sharing saves costs. Remember to communicate, cooperate, and share!
- Investigate the possibility of using security practices, strategies, and technology for core business processes!

ALL GOOD RELATIONSHIPS RELY ON EFFECTIVE COMMUNICATION

I have been outlining the importance of communication throughout this book. We are often so blinded by the abilities of technology that we forget that every relationship mostly relies on simple communication. The success of the security function, and consequently, the success of its security strategies starts with its ability to interact with decision makers, efficiently present them the benefits of security and completely understand their directions and business objectives. Second, communication is the most important tool for getting each person in the organization to become an active part in its security efforts. Naturally, we also deter potential perpetrators by communicating our security firmness. Finally, by linking security to our products and service and communicating the feeling of being secure to our customers, we grow the appeal of our products and services, boost our reputation, and strengthen consumer confidence (see Chapter 1: Commercial Security Challenges: *A Historical Perspective*; Chapter 2: Security and Economics: *From Global Causes to Local Circumstances*; Chapter 3: About Corporate Security: *The Function, its Philosophies, and Practices*; Chapter 4: Risk: *Stuck Between Security and Economics*; Chapter 5: Quantifying Incidents: *Rethinking Loss*; Chapter 6: Quantifying Information Security: *Calculating the Intangible*; Chapter 7: Influencing Performance: *Running an Efficient Security Organization*; Chapter 8: Costs Saving and Cost Avoidance: *Security as the Usual Suspect*; Chapter 9: Security Outsourcing: *A Double-Edged Sword*; Chapter 10: Resilience—*The Wider Concept of Security*; Chapter 11: Marketing and Security: *The Appeal of Target Hardening*; Chapter 12: Sales Potential of Security: *Security as Ingredient of the Product*; Chapter 13: Security Metrics: *Measuring Performance*; Chapter 14: Security Inventions: *Security Technology in Business Analytics*).

Index

Printed in the United States
By Bookmasters